New Year's Day

New Year's Day
at the Hotel Australia

Lindsay Barrett

PUNCHER & WATTMANN

First published in 2019

Published by Puncher and Wattmann
PO Box 279
Waratah NSW 2298

http://www.puncherandwattmann.com
puncherandwattmann@bigpond.com

ISBN 9781922186720

A catalogue record for this book is available
NATIONAL from the National Library Australia.
LIBRARY
OF AUSTRALIA

Cover design by Sophie Gaur
Typesetting by Christine Bruderlin
Printed by Lightning Source

Australian Government

Australia Council for the Arts

This project has been assisted by the Australian
Government through the Australia Council, its
arts funding and advisory body.

Skyscraper
(MLC Tower)

The liftride drags you by your power breakfast
up and on to ever higher echelons
of Total Personal Achievement,
and from ground zero you arrive
half a century of storeys skywards
for the cool, unruffled kill on this
most level playing field you call success.

Peter Kirkpatrick (1996)

Contents

1. A Century of Progress

In 1937 Fowler Potteries in Marrickville celebrated one hundred years of operations. Fowler's was one of the oldest industrial concerns in Australia. Enoch Fowler, a potter from County Tyrone in Ireland, had arrived in New South Wales in 1836 and founded the company within a year. A century later Fowler's creation commemorated both its origins and its corporate personality by issuing each of its employees an ashtray in the form of a miniature nineteenth-century pottery kiln. In those days my father Arthur was an apprentice potter at Fowler's, and he duly received one of these model kilns glazed in the rich shade of green that is the hallmark of Fowlerware. He kept this curiously inelegant little model all his life, mixed in amongst the surviving bits and pieces from his own subsequent career in pottery.

Arthur had taken up his apprenticeship after leaving school. It had been an easy transition. From playing with his schoolmates in the playground he'd moved on to larking about with his fellow apprentices at the pottery works, joking over a cuppa at morning tea, getting the cricket bat and ball out for a bit of a hit at lunchtime. These were the all too brief good years. The Great War was a memory, the Great Depression almost over, and Australia was still far from the shadow cast over Europe by Hitler and Stalin, and from Japan's merciless war against China. There was at this time a re-emerging sense of national optimism, and perhaps this is what led Arthur and three of his workmates to make an audacious pledge. Perhaps it was also a sense of historical continuity and permanence fostered by Fowler's one hundred years of productivity, which was after all an impressive record in a nation that was itself only a century and a half old, that also inspired their pledge. For, over their cup of tea one morning, Arthur and three of his mates vowed that regardless of whatever directions the roads of life took them, they would meet again at the start of the next century, at midday on New Year's Day of the year 2000 at the Hotel Australia, in central Sydney on the corner of Rowe and Castlereagh streets.

This really was an ambitious vow: the date set for the reunion was more than sixty years into an unknown future, and these young fellows were already fifteen years old. Within two years Australia would be engaged in another war: a war that would at one point seem to threaten the very existence of the nation, a war in which the young pottery apprentices would be compelled to serve. And if they survived this war, they would then face more mundane though equally taxing struggles against banks and bureaucracies, as they battled to run small businesses while building homes, raising children, and maintaining marriages. But in 1937 they were unaware of any of this; all these events lay in an unknown future, the property of both a personal and national destiny. And yet the young potters seem to have possessed such cheerful faith that all would be well. For this is what their pledge displayed: a simple, robust belief in the future and in their own place within it.

What fascinates me most about this pledge is the sense of permanence underpinning it, the brash assumption by these boys that their lives would continue unchecked and unchallenged across this great gulf of time, an assumption fuelled at heart by a belief in the ideal of progress, an ideal that in turn informed a nation incapable of perceiving itself as anything other than young. Now it is true that on one level this faith in the future as a space in which one has their own rightful place was simply a product of the passions and enthusiasms of youth. The young – in particular, perhaps, young white men in a country like Australia – tend to view the future as a limitless field of possibilities and goals, rather than as the slow and jumbled procession of minor achievements, thwarted desires and dashed hopes that life often turns out to be.

At the same time though, this fusion of the ideals of national and personal progress exemplified by the apprentice potters' pledge was also very much a product of its place and time. In Australia, in the early to mid twentieth century, progress and a faith in the future formed what was perhaps *the* defining national creed. Born of British imperialism and the European Enlightenment, Australia had also been born into modernity, and within nineteenth and twentieth century modernity social and technological progress was the driving force. As the nation grew into its designated place within the Empire, it was widely felt that there would always be newer and better machines, newer and better markets, newer and better ways of doing things, and in Australia there would always be more land to develop, more resources to exploit, more blank spaces on the map to be filled in. So, the late 1930s were auspicious years for the commemoration not just of the longevity of Fowler's, but in relation to the bigger picture of Australia's national destiny. 1938 began with celebrations in January marking the one hundred and fiftieth anniversary of the first act in the British invasion and occupation of the continent. In Sydney, one million people (more than one tenth of the nation's population) lined the streets to watch a parade celebrating the landing of Captain Phillip and his marines and convicts at Sydney Cove in 1788.

It is no surprise that in such a climate these young apprentices, enmeshed as they were in the workings of a venerable industrial concern located near the heart of this large and prosperous city, should have displayed such a faith in the continuity of their social and political world. There was though a paradox at play here, for if the experience of modernity was grounded in the ideal of progress, then it was an experience not of permanence and stability but of continual transformation. In social, industrial and technological terms, progress wasn't about building and maintaining, it was about building, and then demolishing, and then building again, with the very products of modern society always ripe for replacement by the next version, the next model, the next way of doing things.

Modernity was always working on exceeding itself.[1] And the consequences of this are responsible for the paradox at the heart of the apprentice potters' pledge: it was the very forces of progress that allowed them to project themselves so far into the future and across such radically transforming social and cultural terrain, while at the same time fostering the assumption that, despite these seemingly unstoppable forces of mechanistic change, Australia would, for white men like themselves, remain essentially the same. In other words, while they hoped that in sixty years' time they would still be alive, they also assumed that in sixty years the Australia they knew so well would still exist, changed and yet somehow unchanged. And ironically, this is exactly where the pledge failed, because on New Year's Day in the year 2000, the very location for their meeting, the Hotel Australia, no longer existed. It had been demolished in 1972 to make way for a completely new structure that was (briefly) Australia's tallest building, the monolithic concrete tower of the MLC Centre on Martin Place.

*

Given the degree of emotional investment many Australians who lived through the 1950s and 1960s have in understanding the time as a golden era of prosperity and stability, it may seem discourteous to assert that this period was really only one particular, limited interval of a certain kind of economic growth. Essentially, though, that's what

4

I want to do. Yet I do not want to examine this period of our history in broad terms – the wide sweep of global economic transformation, and the international political realignments that both underpinned and resulted from these transformations – but from the point of view of the actual experience of such change: from ground level, from the point of view of these events that, schooner of Reschs in hand, one had from the Long Bar of the Hotel Australia.

In the mid 1960s Hannah Arendt wrote an essay on the work of Walter Benjamin, which later became the introduction to an English translation of a collection of Benjamin essays, *Illuminations*. There is a passage in Arendt's piece that I find myself coming back to again and again, every time I lose my theoretical way. Arendt is writing about Benjamin writing about Charles Baudelaire. In his analysis of Baudelaire and nineteenth-century Paris, Arendt sees Benjamin as captivated by 'the correlation between a street scene, a speculation on the stock exchange, a poem, a thought, with the hidden line which holds them together', the line that, in fact, enables the historian to 'recognize that they must all be placed in the same period'. Benjamin, Arendt continues, was aiming to capture a portrait of history 'in the most insignificant representations of reality, its scraps, as it were'.[2]

My fascination with this passage began even before I really understood what it meant, or what the implications for such a project were, and certainly long before I understood why Theodor Adorno sternly criticised Benjamin's approach for its 'wide-eyed' obsession with the details rather than the structure of the defining currents of history and experience.[3] Yet from Benjamin's point of view, as Arendt points out, it was only the half-forgotten and insignificant bits and pieces of the 'everyday' that actually provided any kind of access to the otherwise silent mechanisms of history. For Benjamin, it was the very 'spirit' of an age that came together with its 'material manifestation' in the architecture of ordinary everyday life.

If this was true of nineteenth-century Paris, then I think it was also true of twentieth-century Sydney, or for that matter any other place that has been part of the modern experience. Naturally enough, though, in a different place and at a different time, the correlations and the important elements are different too. Street scenes, poems and speculations on the stock exchange are all vital ingredients of any modern story, but in this story I want to focus on some different objects – novels, football, skyscrapers, and shopping centres – for these are some of the ingredients that made up the Australian experience of the 1950s and 1960s.

Most of Benjamin's objects of analysis could be found in Paris, while the objects in my story mostly come from Sydney, and it is a fair criticism that the Sydney experience is not the be all and end all of the Australian experience of this period. Nonetheless, as one of Australia's two biggest cities, and thereby one of the nation's main points of interaction with the rest of the world, it was Sydney, along with Melbourne, which most quickly responded to and was most dramatically affected by the great upheavals of the time. And besides, it's also the one place I know best.

These years in question, the two to three decades following the Second World War, saw the most dramatic social and cultural transformations experienced in twentieth-century Australia. Indeed, they rank with the European invasion of the continent at the end of the 1700s and the discovery and exploitation of gold deposits in the 1850s and 1860s as one of the three key periods of transformation in which the very social fabric of Australia was remade. In 1945 Australia had a population of 7 million overwhelmingly Anglo-Celtic people, and its GDP was A£1.5 billion. Three decades later this population had more than doubled and was decidedly multicultural, while GDP was A$33 billion.[4] At the same time, building on the armaments industry created during the Second World War, during these decades Australia

6

also became comprehensively industrialised, finding itself no longer just a market for, but now an independent producer of, numerous forms of consumer and industrial goods. Concurrent with this period of industrial development, and inseparably associated with it, came the massive expansion of suburbia and the final transformation of agrarian Australia into one of the world's most urbanised cultures.

These are the historical-cultural processes that are the background to the objects and characters and experiences I want to look at: the skeins of asphalt reaching out across the vacant, clear-felled hills and plains surrounding the old city and its rows of nineteenth-century terraces; the immigrant concreters and bricklayers sweating it out under the relentless summer sun and the cloud-empty deep blue sky; the Holdens and Falcons crammed into the colour-coded stacks of the decked car park attached to the all-enclosed, climate-controlled, ultra-modern shopping centre; the whirring, flashing, ravenous banks of poker machines laid out across the gaudy carpet of the brick and tile palace of the Leagues club; the ferro-concrete towers spreading their corporate might and midday shadows across the narrow lanes and forgotten bars where larrikin poets once drank themselves into oblivion.

As a guide through his analysis of the streets of nineteenth-century Paris, Benjamin chose the allegorical figure of the *flâneur*, the celebrated 'botaniser of the asphalt', the bohemian chronicler and philosopher of the crowded metropolis of high modernity.[5] But I want to ask a very different figure to lead us through the suburbs of the Great Australian Dream. I call him the self-made man – the small businessman, the self-employed tradesman, the master of the quarter-acre block who was responsible for so much of the rebuilding and recreation of the nation in those postwar decades. As we shall see, just like the *flâneur*, the self-made man was also a marker of his times, and, in his own way, he was also a philosopher, although it has

7

to be admitted that he was no botaniser, he didn't step back to study his landscape. Rather, he simply got on with the job of building his world, often from scratch, with whatever was at hand.

Like all textual devices, the self-made man is a cipher, not an actual person. But like all historical tropes he is also a figurative representation of an actual human subject: real people really did play these roles, and hold down these jobs: ordinary, everyday men who laid the bricks and poured the concrete that made the postwar nation of Australia. While a complete history of the self-made man in Australia is still to be written, his most comprehensive portrait can be found in the pages of John O'Grady's 1957 populist classic, *They're a Weird Mob*, a book that sold a quarter of a million copies within three years of its publication, a book that told a simple story about a group of self-employed builders and bricklayers. Plain, almost cartoonish though it may appear, even a brief glance through O'Grady's book, not to mention its sequels, provides the reader with a detailed illustration of both the figure in question as well as his times. The ideals of building, of making progress, of putting the past behind you, are present on almost every page. It is no surprise the books were so successful, as it is doubtful if anything ever written in this country has spoken so directly or immediately to such a large segment of the population.

I still remember how annoyed I felt on first reading in Leonie Kramer's introduction to the 1981 *Oxford History of Australian Literature*, that unlike 'Literature', 'popular writing' was not an object worthy of serious study. Such reactionary, stuffed-shirt silliness would itself be unworthy of a reply were it not for the all damage that it, and the other forms of elitism that dominated Australian literary and cultural criticism for most of the twentieth century, have done. For, aside from narrowing the minds of a couple of generations of students, teachers and bureaucrats, in its wake this critical orthodoxy also inspired its opposite: an equally effective, in terms of its power to assume a position of analytic dominance, and equally banal, form of cultural studies divorced from the discipline's original political grounding.

What I want to do is to allow the figure of the self-made man to guide us on a path between both of these critical extremes. For the self-made man was just as likely to be found hard at work in one of Patrick White's Nobel Prize-winning novels as he was in a John O'Grady homage to the heroes of the battle for brick veneer. He was also equally at home entertaining legions of fans on the rugby league field, or driving the family to the brand new suburban shopping centre on a Saturday morning. For the cultural forces that the self-made man embodied sprang from the deepest currents of power running through the nation, and to this extent they transcended, even as they worked to define, class and gender and race relations. At the same time, the voice of the self-made man also found a clear, dominant place within the particular economic order underpinning everyday life.

This is a *man's story*, and in selecting the figure of the self-made *man* to serve as a representative of and guide to the era, I'm also aware that concentrating on him runs the risk of further marginalising the experiences of Australian women of the period. However, it is quite simply the case that the majority of published accounts of Australian life during the 1950s and 1960s were overwhelmingly composed from the point of view of men. Nor, by the way, is there anything new about such an observation: the past few decades of feminist historiography and cultural analysis have clearly demonstrated the pervasive gender bias consistently at work in the production of our literary and historical record. Similarly, the figure of the solidly heterosexual self-made man is also tied to a restrictive ethnic category, initially that of the English-speaking Anglo-Celt, though it was progressively expanded to include a range of European ethnicities too. Indeed, the impact of the great postwar immigration project, and its transformation of our understanding of national character and identity, is a crucial part of the story of the self-made man.

To stress the point, though: in using the figure of the self-made man as a representative of the era I'm not trying to suggest that the man who occupied this position within the social field was some sort of archetypal Australian with a privileged access to and a definitive claim on Australian experience and identity. In fact, I want to argue quite the opposite: that the reification of this particular character during the 1950s and 1960s worked (naturally enough) to position his experience as central to that of the overall national experience. As already mentioned, this had two dramatic effects. Firstly, it tended to marginalise, or at least subordinate, the experiences of those Australians who didn't fit into this particular category. Secondly, as this character was bound up with small business capitalism, it also allowed an effortless coupling of a conservative understanding of national identity with the chief form of economic organisation at the time. In other words, it is the self-made man who, if we spend a little time deconstructing his character and activities, can provide us with some important insights into this period of our history and culture so crucial to our experience of Australia in the early twenty first century.

*

I first remember my father telling me about his proposed reunion with the Fowler's apprentices when I was about seven or eight years old, at the end of the 1960s. Perhaps I could drive him down to the Hotel Australia on the day, I recall him musing, after all, by then he'd probably be too old to drive himself, and I'd be forty years old and no doubt I'd have a car of my own. I don't remember him passing comment on the fate of the pledge when the hotel was demolished a few years later, though I'm sure he must have said something. Over the course of the next three decades he mentioned the pledge less frequently. Eventually, he seemed to lose interest in it altogether. Occasionally I'd bring the subject up, suggesting other possible venues for the meeting, but I was unable to propose anywhere that interested him. And by this stage he'd lost contact with the other apprentices; he didn't even know if they were still alive. Anyway, it didn't matter, because with the passing of the Hotel Australia so too had passed the reunion plans of the Fowler Potteries centenary apprentices.

For a long time I couldn't understand why he had completely lost interest in this reunion planned so many years before. After all, he'd seemed keen on the meeting when I was a boy, and this was at least thirty years after having first agreed to it. Yet now, it seemed, he'd just as firmly let go of the idea. Why not just find somewhere else to meet up with his mates from long ago, I wondered? Surely it was the date that was the major milestone to be commemorated, affirming as it did the achievement of having lived out a life across the long twentieth century.

But what I had totally failed to appreciate in my problem solver's desire to find another location for the reunion was the central place of the Hotel Australia in the cultural and social geography of Sydney, and Australia, for those of Arthur's generation. For the Hotel Australia was the epitome of style and sophistication and yet at the same time it was a public place rather than a club or a private enclave, the focal point of a number of strata of public culture. It was the meeting place of meeting places, and in this sense it was irreplaceable, for when it passed so too passed, for those to whom it mattered and for those who had lived it, a particular way of life. There was no point meeting somewhere else, because the way of life the reunion had been designed to affirm no longer existed. Progress, which had created this way of life in the first place, had now literally eaten it up.

2. The Work of Art

A few years ago I was sifting through piles of books in a second-hand bookshop in Camberwell in south London. In the £1 throwaway bin I found an early hardback edition of Patrick White's *Voss* in reasonable condition. I had been collecting first editions of twentieth-century Australian fiction for quite a while, and finding this copy of *Voss* made me mildly excited. It wasn't the 1957 edition, it was the third reprint of 1958 but, I reasoned, its presence suggested that perhaps there were real treasures hidden away somewhere in the jumble of this shop. I held it up, its dust jacket bearing Sidney Nolan's minimalist blue, black and white cartoon of a grizzly, bespectacled, middle-aged man in a hat, and asked the shop owner if she had anything else like it. 'I'm not sure,' she replied, 'the humour section is against the back wall. Perhaps you should have a look there.'

I was momentarily lost for words. What was she saying, this member of the upper segment of Britain's lower middle class? That Australian literature was a joke? Or merely that she thought Patrick White was laughable, and that his tortured, long-winded antipodean parables were best classified under the same label as the works of John Cleese and Spike Milligan. In the course of the few seconds of silence hanging between us I quickly realised my mistake: I had yet again fallen into the trap of assuming that the rest of the world knows as much about Australia as we are forced to know about it. For it wasn't at all the case that this woman thought the works of Patrick White hilarious; she had, in fact, never heard of either White or *Voss*, and had assumed from the cover art that the book in question must be some sort of comic novel. Such confusion was, I assured her, fair enough, as all Patrick White had ever done was win the Nobel Prize for Literature in 1973. She made no reply and simply stared at me in a vaguely hostile fashion, which was understandable, as this particular English class faction never takes to irony too well. So I handed over a pound and departed with *Voss*, without bothering to peruse the humour section at the back.

Now I was back out on the frozen street, the merits and significance of Australia's greatest modernist painter and greatest modernist writer having been dismissed in one sharp exchange. What to do? Where to go to sort out my thoughts? I proceeded to the pub on the corner and had a pint, and flicked through the pages of the musty old *Voss*, looking for my favourite passage, the one in which Voss gives Dugald (who has been guiding him through a landscape that to the German is an increasingly destructive wilderness) a last letter to take back to his muse, Laura. Dugald never delivers this letter. Instead, he eventually tears it into shreds, allowing 'the sad thoughts, the bad, the thoughts that were too heavy, or in any way hurtful', of which the German had so obviously been keen to rid himself, to flutter away on the breeze.[6]

Perhaps I shouldn't be too hard on this clueless Englishwoman in the bookshop, as even White himself found Nolan's cover art for *Voss* 'disappointing' when it was first shown to him.[7] Despite his

13

misgivings that it trivialised the character of Johann Ulrich Voss, he ultimately approved the use of the sketch, an image of a 'fat amiable botanist' as he put it, on the book's cover.[8] This was mainly because he had such great respect for Sidney Nolan (with whom he was developing a famous though fraught friendship) as an artist. For White, the *Voss* cover was infinitely preferable to the cover art for his previous book *The Tree of Man*.

The Tree of Man was the novel that had finally made White's reputation as a writer, even if it was a reputation destined not to live on into the twenty first century among British booksellers. In a masterful display of imperial indifference, for the jacket of *The Tree of Man* White's publishers, Eyre & Spottiswoode, had commissioned a sketch of a group of gum trees by an amateur painter who worked at Australia House. As a largely unknown Australian author, White had to accept the image even though he didn't like it. But the subsequent success of the book had increased his clout considerably with his publishers. And so, when it came to *Voss*, White was in the position to both insist to Eyre & Spottiswoode that they accept Nolan as the jacket artist, and to convince Nolan that he should accept the job.

White's scrupulous biographer David Marr refers to the cover art for *The Tree of Man* as 'a drab mess', which it is.[9] Yet in terms of the novel's content, the subject matter of the painting (eucalypts), is reasonably appropriate. Or at least it is halfway there. If White's literary successes had come earlier and he'd been in the position to insist on using the work of an iconic Australian painter for *The Tree of Man*, just as he was for *Voss*, then I'd suggest that, thematically at least, Frederick McCubbin's *The Pioneer* would have provided a particularly suitable image.

McCubbin's iconic triptych has been on display at the National Gallery of Victoria since its purchase in 1906. This was some two years after McCubbin finished the picture, but it had taken the Gallery that long to push the fee down to half his original asking price, in spite of the fact that the *Age* newspaper was hailing the painting as 'an irrefutable demonstration that Australia can produce a strong and beautiful national art of her own'.[10] Indeed, as the *Age* saw it, the triptych format enabled McCubbin 'to give pictorial insight into three episodes in the life history of those strong spirits who opened up this Continent'.[11]

While it may have received a solemn reception in the Federation years, these days *The Pioneer* bears distinct overtones of colonial kitsch. The three panels show in turn: a pioneer making a camp in the bush while his young wife sits in the foreground wistfully dreaming of the civilised life she has left behind; the pioneer sitting on the stump of large tree he has recently felled, axe beside him, wife with babe in arms before him, and bush cottage in the background; finally, in the third panel a young man inspects a bush gravesite while a glittering Turneresque city shimmers through the trees in the far distance. As per the conventions of the triptych form, it is the central panel that is the centerpiece of the narrative, with those on either side providing the before and after moments in this story of the conquest of the bush by the hand of a strong but humble man.

McCubbin had borrowed the triptych format from European religious art, and to an extent there is a direct parallel with the works of Patrick White, for whom quasi-Christian themes and their manifestations in the great emptiness of Australia was also a great concern. I'm less interested here though in this similarity than in the comparable thematic content of the two men's works. For I'd argue that *The Pioneer* is far more suitable as an accompaniment to *The Tree of Man* than the work of the nameless 1950s Australia House artist, because it doesn't just show a stand of gum trees, it shows a man in the process of applying productive violence to a stand of gum trees. It was just this sort of image that grounded White's celebrated novel.

To illustrate my point, I suggest we take a look at the opening passage of *The Tree of Man*:

> A cart drove between the two big stringybarks and stopped. These were the dominant trees in that part of the bush, rising above the scrub with the simplicity of true grandeur. So the cart stopped, grazing the hairy side of a tree, and the horse, shaggy and stolid as the tree, sighed and took root.[12]

This is art, not just description, or so the aesthetic argument goes. And it *is* a beautiful piece of imagery, as well as a demonstration of the sort of stylistic mastery that would later win its author his much-deserved Nobel Prize. There is however always more to writing than just style, even if that style registers at the level of beauty. But to repeat my first point: it *is* a beautiful piece of writing. Yet even this assertion is the product of a particular style of critical apprehension of the text. Why is it beautiful? Because when I read it I don't read it in a vacuum, I read it against everything else I've ever read, and I judge it, implicitly, against a mode of text-making I've *learned* to recognise as good, or even great. Yet the fundamental point is, I've learned to read this way, just like I've learned every other form of behaviour I engage in, and there is nothing transhistorical or transcendent or eternal about the experience. Ultimately this is just a piece of writing, written in a particular place and at a particular time, read by someone else, in another place at another time.

It is becoming increasingly unfashionable to mention him these days, but I can never look over this opening passage of *The Tree of Man* without thinking of Michel Foucault, and of the recklessly precise manner in which he would pull apart whatever cultural text took his fancy. Central to his approach was the route by which, in any given society, the really important concepts and ideas always find their way into the important texts and objects of culture. This was an idea Foucault had inherited from Karl Marx but, influenced just as much by Friedrich Nietzsche, he opened it up to include a broad spectrum of powers and forces rather than simply those formations dictated by economics, like ownership, class, and access to capital.

So what would Foucault have thought of this opening passage of *The Tree of Man*? Well, he might have said that it embodied a very European romanticist, colonialist and maybe even masculinist approach to the object it proposed to describe – a particular piece of Australian bush. White doesn't just tell us there are trees at this place, Foucault might have said, instead he tells us that the trees are 'dominant trees', and that they have the 'simplicity of true grandeur'. These are powerful markers of hierarchy and key elements in a practice of ordering, two conceptual technologies that were crucial to the European apprehension and possession of indigenous landscapes across the world. To put it simply, seeing particular elements of the landscape as dominant allowed an appreciation of the landscape as not only dominated but open to further domination, the domination of Man, a conception that was at the very heart of the European colonial project. Similarly, the ontological status of these trees is beyond dispute; they are said to be simply truly grand, a definition that appeals to a transcendental, pre-social category of truth that then serves to support, and to negate criticism of, alternative opinions.

To repeat my earlier point: none of this means that the passage is not a beautiful and enduring piece of writing, but it does mean that its beauty has been created not just through crafting words but by deploying some very powerful ideas. Let us continue with White's opening for this novel: the cart is carrying a man, who is accompanied by his dog as well as his horse. He gets down from the cart:

> Then the man took an axe and struck at the side of a hairy tree, more
> to hear the sound than for any other reason. And the sound was cold
> and loud. The man struck the tree, and struck, till several white chips
> had fallen. He looked at the scar in the side of the tree. The silence was

17

immense. It was the first time anything like this had happened in that part of the bush.

He then hobbles his horse and continues with his work:

> The man made a lean-to with bags and a few saplings. He built a fire. He sighed at last, because the lighting of his small fire had kindled in him the first warmth of content. Of being somewhere. That particular part of the bush had been made his by the entwining fire. It licked at and swallowed the loneliness.

This is why, this originary scene of possession-taking, of initiating the process of domination of 'that part of the bush', I nominated McCubbin's *The Pioneer* as a suitable piece of cover art for the book. Not that subsequent editions have followed this line: as a designated literary modernist, the cover images for White's books have generally been drawn (once he became a bestseller anyway) from modernist painting and imagery, like the *Voss* example. However, if we relate the central theme of the book backwards towards its grounding in Australian cultural history, then the similarities seem obvious, as *The Tree of Man* is also a story about a pioneer, albeit one without the excesses of myth and melancholia that imbue McCubbin's painting.

One reason White's vision was a lot sharper and more critically aware than McCubbin's was that, apart from the fact he was working five decades, two world wars and a calamitous economic slump later, he'd not really set out to compose a heroic account of the struggle of the pioneer. Rather, as he put it at the time, the aim of the book was 'to discover the extraordinary in the ordinary, the mystery and poetry which alone could make bearable the lives of ordinary men and women'.[13] The premise of *The Tree of Man* was based directly on White's own life with his partner Manoly Lascaris on their small farm at Castle Hill, on what in those days was the rural fringe of north-western Sydney. David Marr details how a somewhat despondent White had originally begun the manuscript as 'A Life Sentence on

Earth'. Once he saw that it was working, though, and that as a novel it may actually have some merit, his mood lifted, he became more enthusiastic about it, and he gave it a more positive title.[14]

White's chief concern in *The Tree of Man*, as with Tolstoy's in *War and Peace*, centres on the individual's struggle with the enigma of existence. White wanted *The Tree of Man* to illustrate the immanence of the Spirit, the way, as he saw it, God was literally a part of everything, even the sky and the trees and the earth. Simultaneously, he also used the novel to explore the struggles of marriage and domestic partnership, and of the everyday joy and awfulness contained therein. The vehicle for these explorations is the story of Stan Parker, the most common of common men. Stan, as we have seen in the passage quoted above, arrives with his horse and cart in an empty, untouched (at least by European hands), piece of bush. He sets up camp, cuts down some trees, builds himself a shack, goes away, finds a wife and brings her back, builds up a farm, develops friendships with the growing local community of people much like himself, goes and fights in the First World War, has two children, buys a car, finds himself increasingly built out by the encroachments of suburbia, and eventually sees his surname become the name by which this place he has pioneered is known.

This is a common Australian story, but it is important to remember that it isn't the only Australian story. What we get with Stan Parker is an image of a particular form of masculinity combined with a particular form of entrepreneurial skill. Stan might be a common man but he is also a reified stereotype, a mid twentieth-century successor to those great Aussie archetypes: the bushman and the digger. Indeed, White's Stan Parker is a remarkable figure within the history of Australian fiction in that he manages to fill all of these key roles: he starts out as a bushman, serves in the Great War as a digger, and then grows into an archetype of that resourceful pioneer of suburbia, the self-made man.

Not that White, who went on to give his fictional outer suburbs and towns names like Baranugli and Budgiwank, was any fan of what he saw as the crass vulgarity of suburbia, or of the practices of suburb building. He liked Castle Hill bucolic and semi-rural, as it was when he arrived there in 1948, rather than as the bland postwar suburb it had become by the time he moved away to inner city Centennial Park in 1964. Stan Parker doesn't like the creeping sprawl of suburbia either. In the later years of his life he comes to regret the way the 'brick homes were in possession' of what he'd once known as bush: 'Deep purple, clinker blue, ox blood, and public lavatory. Here the rites of domesticity were practised, it had been forgotten why, but with passionate, regular orthodoxy'.[15]

Be that as it may, Stan had actually started it all on the day he went out there and got stuck into that first big stringybark with his axe. Subsequently, however much he and Patrick White may have regretted it, everything that happened in the area from that point on was just more of the same process: of tree-felling, land-clearing, and reckless development, first for small farms, then for quarter-acre blocks, and finally for McMansions and indoor furnishing and electrical appliance superstores, for whatever, in fact, there was a dollar in at the time.

But White was not interested in chronicling the building of suburbia, he was concerned instead with creating a parable that reflected on what metaphysically-inclined literary critics liked to call 'universal human experience'. And to this end he largely succeeded. The conservative poet and academic Vincent Buckley, for example, praised *The Tree of Man* for the ingeniously poetic manner in which it placed universal human characters in a uniquely Australian setting.[16] Even the left-leaning novelist Marjorie Barnard declared in *Meanjin* that

The Tree of Man 'tells with infinite quietness the story of ordinary people'.[17]

This was nevertheless only one shade of opinion. Writing in the Marxist journal *Overland*, the tireless social realist Katharine Susannah Prichard argued that there was nothing universal about White's writing, it was just a bourgeois deception full of 'style and tricks in the use of words which appeal to sophisticated readers'.[18] This is an important point – the class-based nature of a novel such as *The Tree of Man* – and I'll come back to it in later chapters. For the moment though I want to return to this notion of Stan Parker's life representing a form of universal human experience, or rather, in a less lofty fashion, universal Australian experience.

The reification of Stan is a great example of the way national stereotypes work. To put it crudely, a particular lifestyle and a particular set of beliefs and social and cultural practices come to be closely associated with a particular type of character and individual, and this character type then becomes representative of national experience in general. The particular lifestyles and character types that become the national stereotypes are the ones that best represent the really powerful social and cultural forces of their time. Thus the image of the convict in his ragged pyjamas has come to define the first decades of life in the Australian colonies despite the fact that Indigenous Australians vastly outnumbered him. Similarly, the swagman and the bushie represent the Australia of the late nineteenth century, despite the fact that by this point in time the majority of Australians lived in cities, and the work of urban wharf labourers, for example, was just as important as that of shearers, as the nation could only ride on the sheep's back as far as the docks from which wool was exported. Finally, the Gallipoli digger stands as the representative of the period in which the federation and merger of the colonies into a unified modern nation was affirmed by participation in the Great War, even though Australia was alone among the combatants in not conscripting its servicemen and, consequently, more men actually stayed home than went to war.

To be sure, it is often the point at which the efficacy of such archetypes is peaking, or even in decline, that they flourish most fully and effectively as national icons. Gilberto Freyre demonstrated this very clearly in his studies of the cultural resonance of colonial plantation life in the society and architecture of nineteenth and twentieth century Brazil.[19] Though ethnically and socially different from Brazil, Australia also shared a similar historical trajectory as a nation moving from a colonial to postcolonial place in the world, and so certain aspects of cultural formation were common to the two nations. This is why the swagman was popularised in Australia primarily in the 1890s, at a time of increasing urbanisation, and the digger became an iconic figure during the 1920s rather than during the war he fought. This pattern also holds true for the self-made man, who really came to prominence at the end, rather than at the beginning, of the postwar boom.

Patrick White may have been most interested in exploring the experience of a life sentence on earth, but what we also find in *The Tree of Man* – no doubt unintentionally on White's part – is a muted celebration of outer urban development. Perhaps 'celebration' is too strong a word, but nonetheless the will to clear land, to build and to create a space of one's (a man's) own, provides the cultural foundations upon which the tale is played out. And so the key elements of the Australian traditions of progress, development and landscape exploitation remain intact. Indeed, from a less hostile angle than that of Katharine Susannah Prichard, John McLaren, also writing in *Overland*, called for a more sympathetic reception of White's work because, after all, his characters were not that different from Steele Rudd's Dad and Dave.[20]

McLaren was onto something here. In terms of plot, it is not really that far from *On Our Selection* to *The Tree of Man*. The vast gulf of difference lies instead with the way White wrote about his characters, and about what he made them think, not what he made them do. Manning Clark said that Dad Rudd 'had no metaphysical anguish: he was an Australian'.[21] Maybe Clark was right, and this is how it was for the average Australian when the Rudd chronicles were published in 1899. But Stan Parker, modernist product of the 1950s, was 'complex', even though he was also simple and ordinary. In other words, as a literary character he was designed for consumption by, as Prichard had so accurately put it, a 'sophisticated' readership. Yet this was a complexity at the level of character and style, not at the level of setting or action. For what Patrick White wrote about in *The Tree of Man* – a man clearing some land and building a house – was, it seemed in the era of the self-made man, a subject that was just not up for debate: it was simply what Australians did.

3. The Existentialists

In Peter Doyle's urban crime novel *The Devil's Jump* (2001), set in 1946, antihero Billy Glasheen's older brother Ron, recently returned from 'pushing the Japs back yard by yard over the Owen Stanleys', attempts to 'straighten out' his errant younger sibling:

> The next day Ron had me drive him out to Padstow, a sleepy little stop on the East Hills Line. He directed me down a new dirt road which cut through the bush about half a mile from the station, then had me stop at a bend, where a 'for sale' sign was nailed to a gum tree.
>
> Ron got out of the car. 'What do you reckon?' he said.

Ron, it transpires, has bought himself a quarter-acre block of soon-to-be-realised suburban dream. He paces out the spatial dimensions of his imaginary castle, showing Billy where he'll put the house, the garage, the chook shed, and the swing for the children his missus Glenys will produce once they are settled. 'I know it's not much now' he admits to Billy, but 'when they get the sewer in and the roads sealed this will be a good place. Quiet. Clean.' And there are other blocks still for sale, Ron continues, and Billy should get himself one. Ron will even help him out with some capital. 'Sooner or later you're going to want to settle down', he tells him.[22]

So Billy tries to imagine himself in his very own bungalow, reclining in his smoking jacket with pipe and brandy after a hard day's work. And he can almost picture it, almost. Then he heads back to the inner city, to continue collecting rents and emptying gaming machines for publican and racketeer Mick 'Misery' Toohey. Much to Ron's disappointment, this brief visit to Padstow is the closest Billy will ever get to a simple, honest life in the suburbs. As for Ron, well, the *Get Rich Quick* trilogy (of which *The Devil's Jump* is the third volume), follows Billy's ups and downs, not Ron's. Ron is a peripheral figure, and we never do get to find out if he manages to settle down in his dream home with Glenys, and watch the kids play on the swings while drinking Flag Ale on warm summer afternoons. But rest assured, even if Ron didn't achieve his suburban dream, hundreds of thousands of others did.

In the 1950s the Georges River area, with its developing suburbs strung out along the last few stops on the East Hills line, provided as fine an example of postwar Australian suburbia as one could find: a small group of shops clustered around the station, with some of the nearby streets filled up with houses on quarter-acre blocks and other streets made up merely of fenced-in patches of long grass. Meanwhile, the tracts of land on the fringe of the suburb simply stood idle, patiently waiting their turn to be transformed into an image of suburban uniformity courtesy of the products of the Punchbowl Brick and Pipe Company.

Nor were Ron and Billy Glasheen the first Australian literary figures to have made their way out to the Georges River area in search of a little piece of paradise. For it was to one of these nondescript, empty blocks of suburban land that Nino Culotta ventured for his first day's work in the lucky country one hot October morning in 1957, the day after he arrived in Sydney from Italy. Nino is the protagonist of John O'Grady's populist novel *They're a Weird Mob*, and by the time he'd finished that first day of labouring he'd exerted a far greater influence over more Australian readers than just about any fictional character before him.

Fresh off the boat, as the locals said in those days, Nino had answered an advertisement placed in a newspaper by a man named Joe, which read: 'Builders Labourer. Must be strong. Experience not necessary.' Joe had told him to be at Punchbowl station the following day at 7 am. So he set out next morning from his hotel in Kings Cross, taking the train to Punchbowl and then waiting at the station:

> Indeed it was twenty past seven and I was getting irritable, when I heard a voice say, 'You Nino?' Saying 'Yes', I turned, and saw quite a young man, very slim, who wore heavy unpolished boots, dirty khaki shorts, an old blue shirt, and a very dirty old felt hat. He was holding out his hand. I took it and said 'You are Mr. Joe?'
>
> 'Cut the mister matey. 'Ow yer goin mate orright?'[23]

Nino learns quickly. Not only does he rapidly pick up the tricks of the building trade, he also never calls anyone 'mister' again.

In the parlance of the times, Joe was a spec builder. Like hundreds, thousands, of others in his trade working away in Australia's cities, he speculated on the postwar housing boom. He ran a small building company that operated by buying a block of suburban land, building a house on it, and then selling the house and land package on the almost permanently booming housing market. Often such spec builders had two or three projects on the go at once. Joe employed three men on a regular basis: Dennis, Jimmy and Pat, all of them, like Joe, like so many of the members of Australia's working class in the first half of the twentieth century, of Irish Catholic ethnicity, and all of them (it probably goes without saying) Good Blokes. The spring of 1957 found them putting up a simple brick-veneer house on a block of land in Punchbowl.

Nino though was Italian. He may have been Catholic as well, but he was certainly no builder. He was a journalist who had come to Sydney on the promise of a job on an Italian language newspaper, to find on arrival that the company that published the newspaper had collapsed, and that the job no longer existed. How typical of the dagoes, so many readers would have thought: you really can't depend on 'em. But Nino was resourceful enough to immediately start looking for another line of work, since journalism, with his stilted, limited English, was temporarily out of the question. Perhaps it was simply because he was in the right place at the right time – a place where the resourceful man was king and where, it was said, anyone could find work if they really wanted it – but within twenty-four hours, he'd found himself a job working for Joe as a builder's labourer at Punchbowl. No experience necessary, no questions asked.

In reality, of course, Nino was neither a journalist nor a labourer, he was a character in a book: *They're a Weird Mob*, the comic memoirs of an Italian immigrant, Nino Culotta. Yet even this was fiction too. The book was actually written by an Anglo-Celtic Australian, John O'Grady, a hoax effectively kept up as a marketing tool by both O'Grady and his publisher, Ure Smith, for the first few weeks after the book's release. But as well as being a trickster, O'Grady was a man with a brilliant grasp of idiomatic Australian, and an organic desire to chronicle the building of the Australian Dream in the 1950s, a story in which both European immigrants, and the incessant construction of suburban houses, featured prominently.

Let us start with the latter. Home building and selling was at this time one of the key national preoccupations. By 1966, 71 percent of Australians owned their own home or were purchasing one on a finance scheme, a sharp rise from 56 percent in 1947. Open a Friday afternoon or Saturday morning metropolitan newspaper of the era, and you'd find it filled with advertisements for houses and home sites, ranging from individual units, such as the those built by Joe, Nino and the boys, to developments covering whole suburbs. A new, clean and healthy home, it went without saying, was essential to the growth of a new, clean and healthy family and, *en masse*, a new, clean and healthy Australia: solid brick walls, with a paling fence marking out the perimeter of domestic existence.

Just open, for example, the *Daily Telegraph*: 'A Classic Home is the key to your family's future', says an ad for Classic Homes. This was a company that constructed new brick dwellings in two varieties, the *Bel-Air* and the *Southern Cross*, a selection instantly spanning the field of Australian cultural identity from contemporary Californian style to the image of Henry Lawson boiling his billy.[24] Details were split for convenience into 'facts for wives' and 'facts for husbands'. For the missus there was 'the newest kitchen look', 'low-line cupboards', a 'serving bar separate from your kitchen', 'an American-style shower recess and vanity table', and 'an indoor laundry'. For the king of the castle meanwhile there was important technical information, like the fact that the house was made of 'Clarke's texture brick' with a 'full oregon frame', not to mention the fact that there was 'land available everywhere', 'long term loans' and 'reducible interest rates': important data that the man, as breadwinner and cheque signer, would obviously be concerned with. Conveniently, you could 'Inspect Together', though whether this referred to both styles of house or to inspecting as husband and wife is unclear.

This was the material dimension of the background to *They're a Weird Mob,* the building of postwar Australian suburbia, that sprawling expanse of red tile, brick and fibro that ringed the older, more densely-populated centres of Australia's cities. Yet the book was concerned not just with the materiality of urban forms, but also with non-material culture, and the massive social transformation Australia was undergoing as the great postwar immigration program remade the more or less ethnically uniform Anglo and Celtic nation into what would eventually be an exemplar of multiculturalism. Taken together, these two themes of immigration and suburbia seemed to sum up much of the national experience of the 1950s and 1960s, so perhaps it is no surprise that the book made such a tremendous impact.

They're a Weird Mob was published in November 1957; by the middle of 1959 the number of copies sold had passed 200,000. As David Carter has noted, *They're a Weird Mob* sold more copies, more quickly, and over a longer period of time than any other Australian novel prior to Bryce Courtney who, it should be emphasised, was publishing in a greatly expanded market.[25] Also important in an appreciation of the reach of *They're a Weird Mob* is an element of its circulation that is impossible to quantify: the extent to which it was loaned out by purchasers to relatives and friends who did not generally buy books. This is a form of book distribution far from unique to *They're a Weird Mob*, but it's something worth bearing in mind in relation to this particular text, because it means that it may well have reached an audience at least as sizeable again as that which the official figures indicate. No single book of fiction had ever reached so many Australians, nor would any do so again.

Why was this? Well, open *They're a Weird Mob* and read the first page, and this is what you'll find:

Who the hell's Nino Culotta? That's what you asked yourself when you first picked up this book, wasn't it? Well I'm Nino Culotta. My father had me baptised Giovanni — John — well Giovannino is like Johnny, and Nino is an easier way of saying it. Or a lazier way, if you like. The Culotta family is not famous for doing anything the hard way. It is not famous for doing anything. Because as far as I know it doesn't exist. Not in my family, anyway. My family name is something quite different, but I can't use it here. Because this little book is about Australians, and if they knew who wrote it, some of them might put bricks through my windows. My windows cost me a lot of money and perspiration. To have windows you must first have a house, and I built my house with my own two hands and used the sweat of my head. Whenever I had a fiver I bought something, and whenever I had a weekend I built something. Sometimes concrete, sometimes brick, sometimes wood. And all costing plenty. And you know where I am now? I'm sitting outside my house early on Sunday morning, and the sun is just coming through the trees, and a dog is looking at me. In those trees there are kookaburras, and they laugh. Flying amongst those trees there are dollar birds, and they squawk. There are other birds whose names I do not know, but they all talk and the dew is shining on my grass, and I'm glad I built my house here.[26]

It presents itself as a remarkably self-reflexive text. If Nino really was an Italian then maybe one comparison that could perversely be made would be with Italo Calvino's opening lines of *If On A Winter's Night A Traveller* (1979): 'You are about to begin reading Italo Calvino's new novel, *If On A Winter's Night A Traveller*. Relax. Concentrate. Dispel every other thought . . .' and so on.[27] But Nino is not an Italian, he is Australian, he isn't an artist, and he is certainly no postmodernist. *They're a Weird Mob* is instead a populist exercise in entertainment.

Except that *They're a Weird Mob* is much more as well, and to assert it is simply entertainment is as facile as to assert that *The Tree of Man* is simply a work of art immune to any grubby influences like historical or political context. Because what I find most striking about the opening passage of John O'Grady's book is how similar it is, thematically, to the opening of *The Tree of Man*. Sure, O'Grady's narrator doesn't have the style or finesse – as Prichard would have it – of a Patrick White, but he is telling essentially the same story: the story of a man who gets hold of a bit of land and, through his own hard work and toil and not through anyone else's, builds on it a house of his own.

This is what the Australian economy was all about in those days, the middle years of the 1950s. It wasn't about international best practice, or freeing up market forces, or privatisation, or wrecking the trade union movement (even though the seeds of all of these things would soon be planted), it was about an individual bloke having a go and making what he could out of whatever he could get his hands on. This was the master narrative of the time, but an old-fashioned factor as simple and straightforward as the class system dictated that O'Grady and White represented it in very different ways. Not that they chose these differing modes of expression like you would choose a shirt: they were chosen for them. The way they each expressed themselves was a product of their educations, family backgrounds, and life experiences. O'Grady was, as they said in those days, an ordinary bloke who wrote for ordinary, mostly working-class people, while White was upper class, and wrote for people who were more often than not middle and upper class as well.

I don't want to valorise either of these positions, or try to argue that one is noble and honest and in touch with real life while the other is out of touch, pretentious and elitist. Rather, I'm trying to point out that they tell their stories in very different ways to very different audiences. And I'm also trying to point out that, while they do tell their stories very differently, they still tell essentially the same story, because this was the story of Australia at the time. They do it so differently from each other because they are both working with very different quantities and forms of what the sociologist Pierre Bourdieu called 'cultural capital'. But cultural capital is something I'll come back to later. For the moment, I want to leave aside *The Tree of Man* and keep reading *They're a Weird Mob*.

*

Decades after its heyday *They're a Weird Mob* still resists attempts to pigeonhole it in Australian social and cultural history. Have its effects been progressive and productive, opening up a textual space within which the previously narrow social strictures of Anglo-Celtic Australia mixed with those of southern Europe to re-form as a tolerant, culturally diverse entity? Or is it essentially reactionary, a conservative exercise in containment, and a tactical occupation of the speaking position of the immigrant other on behalf of the paranoid voice of the dominant ethnic group? Actually, the reason *They're a Weird Mob* is so difficult to assess is because it produced both of these effects together, and so remains both an open *and* a closed text. If it was progressive in reaching out towards the immigrant other, it was also conservative in attempting to limit and control the meaning of that gesture. Perhaps such contradictions are inherent in any text that achieves iconic status in a pluralist liberal democracy, where a 'common sense' notion of consensus is the guiding rule of thumb.

Added to these complexities is the fact that the book wasn't just a one-off phenomenon. In the decade after its publication, *They're a Weird Mob* generated something of a minor cultural industry in itself. O'Grady followed it – his first published work – with a string of remarkably successful sequels, initially under the same pseudonym of Nino Culotta, and then under his own name, whilst the phenomenon would eventually culminate in 1966 with the production of a feature film, also titled *They're a Weird Mob*, directed by the brilliantly inconsistent British filmmaker Michael Powell.

On the first page of the novel Nino tells us that his name, Nino, is a strange name for the author of an Australian book. So, the first and perhaps most pressing of the issues confronting the reader is tackled head-on in this first sentence: who is this New Australian? The wariness of the resistant Anglo-Celt, the person for whom the book is ultimately written, is then specifically addressed right from the word go, as is the entire authorial fiction upon which the story is based, with O'Grady's actual name (John, Johnny) even slipped into the equation in a cheeky conceit. Nino is an easy, lazy way of saying it. Remember, we're Australians, and we like to take it easy, though not too easy, we're not loafers or bludgers. We respect a quid, and what a quid can buy, and what it takes to earn it, along with the fact that if you want to sit back and take it easy, you need to get stuck in and have a go first. And there's no doubt that Nino has had a go: he used 'the sweat of [his] head' to build his own house. Not a temple, or a palace, or a towering monument to power, just his own private little castle, of concrete, brick and wood.

The two key themes that both provoke and sustain the story are introduced here, the first being the narrator's composite cultural identity and the second being the practice and processes of building. And in both cases it is the generalised field of social action that is important rather than the specifics. Nino is an Italian immigrant, but his is also a fictional identity standing in for a real one. Similarly, Nino's house is an exemplar of an ideal cultural and material form, rather than a particular dwelling located in a particular place. The real location, assuming there actually is one, is of no consequence. Hence the fact that there are no guides to it, other than those pointing towards a generic, reasonably leafy suburbia: far enough from the city centre to be surrounded by trees full of kookaburras, yet in close enough proximity to the neighbours for its owner to be concerned that if he offends them they may retaliate via a suburban variation on the ancient practice of stoning.

Nino says his book is about Australia. Yet it is not so much a description of the nation as it was at this point in time, as a fictitious memoir describing the process of *becoming* Australian. And to become an Australian, within the logic that dominates the book, is to become one who builds: one who builds a house, a suburb, a city, a nation, one always in the process of *becoming by building*.

This issue of becoming is crucial here. In his later philosophical work Friedrich Nietzsche embraced the concept of Becoming as an empowering, transformative affirmation of existence. Rather than the constraints of Being (the fixed, delineated identity of a stultifying, reactionary society), Becoming, Nietzsche realised, was a process which actually produced freedom, with the subject existing in a perpetually transformative condition, never fixed as This or That, but always in the process of renegotiating existence and identity rather than accepting the constraints and labels of deadening social forces.

This was a particularly liberating concept, especially in the cloying social atmosphere of nineteenth-century bourgeois Europe. But in *They're a Weird Mob* this process is turned on its head, as is the European immigrant, way 'down under' below the equator in twentieth-century Australia. Nino's text is a meditation on Becoming, as he slowly but surely learns the ins and outs of the Australian way. Paradoxically, however, he has as his goal not a permanent state of personal and cultural flux, rather quite the opposite. For Nino's ultimate aim is to arrive and then reside at a final destination. He doesn't want to be forever Becoming Australian, he wants to Be Australian.

It probably goes without saying that Nino's goal was a utopian destination, this domicile of the Real Australian, the place where a man could build his castle and then sit back satisfied without a care in the world and happily watch the birds in the trees. We can call it utopian because it only really existed as a desirable and ostensibly realisable goal due to the confluence of a number of historical, political and economic forces: the geopolitical dynamic that had produced Australia in the first place (one particular manifestation of the European colonial drive), the economic forces that had created the postwar boom, the combination of politics, economics and geography that had led to owner-occupier free-standing brick house suburbia becoming the dominant urban form in Australia, and the historical and political forces that had gendered this seemingly all-pervasive notion of the Australian subject as male. All of these factors produced the precarious, unstable cultural entity of the Australian Dream towards which Nino was drawn.

With the blessing of hindsight, the socially constructed and contingent nature of this national ideal is clear, and yet given the conditions of the time, the postwar boom when everything seemed new and whenever Nino had time on his hands he built something, you could be forgiven for thinking that there was something truly permanent about it all. Such historical, economic and political forces produced a powerful cultural mix for the nation's working and middle classes. As Donald Horne wrote in *The Lucky Country* in 1964, Australians were in possession of 'a strong philosophy of how lives should be led'. The basic outline was as follows:

> You save money and get married; you pay a deposit on a house and furnish it; you hope your children will lead a happier life than you have led; you plan your retirement so that you will enjoy it; and when you die you leave your house to your children so that it can be sold and the money used to pay off the mortgages on their own houses. To ordinary Australians life has its seasons, there are propagation and replacement.[28]

Modest enough aims, but the social and political veracity of such seemingly prosaic materialism shouldn't be underestimated. As Horne went on to observe in his usual vein of educated sarcasm, '"home" occupies as central a position in Australian life as land in a peasant community except that it is disposable after death'.[29] All the same, though, the consolidation of this suburban way of life in Australia coincided with the rise of a well-defined, urbane class of social analysts and critics: men like Horne himself, men much more at home in the refined international circles of modern art and litera- ture than in the functional simplicity of the suburbs.

For Robin Boyd, perpetually disappointed architectural theorist, lover of sophisticated design, and perhaps the most strident of such critics, the physical manifestation of such deeply held beliefs as those expressed by the likes of Nino Culotta (I'm glad I built my house here) produced only a 'dullness', a cultural form 'best represented by the ordinary unit of the pervasive suburbia – the brick-veneer cottage with its asymmetrical double-front and bald plot of often unloved but obligatory garden.'[30] This though is an argument of a different order, that of aesthetics rather than ontology, so ultimately the struggle was really no contest. Because, despite the best defensive efforts of derision and ridicule by the likes of Boyd, Patrick White and Barry Humphries, brick, tile and patio would end up covering most of the inhabited space of the nation.

Little of this highbrow critique registered with the self-made man: he wasn't interested in internationalist issues of style and aesthetics. As Donald Horne saw it, 'Australians often seem to assume that since they leave the world alone it should do the same by them'.[31] Horne describes sitting in a beer garden in Germany and explaining 'the Australian philosophy of life' to a local: 'So' comes the reply, 'you are all Existentialists there!'[32] And, in a practical fashion, this humorous remark was, in truth, a quite exact definition of the organic philosophical underpinnings of postwar suburban Australia.

Indeed, the major cultural and epistemological transformations that had wreaked such havoc on bourgeois France so as to have produced Existentialism – particularly the loss of the moral authority of the church in the face of technological modernity and the inability of the liberal democratic state to fill the gap – had also been at work in Australia, and for a much longer period. The church had been an irrelevance for many Australians for a century or more, while the Great Depression had shown them that there was also no guarantee that the state would always look after them either. And so, while there may have been no Sartre and no Existentialism with a capital E in Australia, in terms of an organic system of belief, there was often a wry acceptance of one's abandonment within a godless universe pervading almost every aspect of everyday life.

At the same time though, in Australia this organic existentialism in no way dovetailed with revolutionary Marxism as it did in Europe. The situation was quite the opposite. Australians weren't prompted by such crises of belief to overthrow existing social structures and make the world anew in Man's, not God's, image. Really, all they wanted was to get by on their own, albeit with a little bit of help from their mates. Transplanted Europeans had been struggling on more or less alone in Australia for a century and a half: struggling to take the land off its Indigenous owners; struggling to survive with no understanding of landscape or climate; struggling to build a modern, technological economy with no capital or infrastructure; struggling to keep Australia white, even though it was on the other side of the world to the place where all the white people lived. White Australians had never really expected God or anyone else to help them. They knew that they were on their own, and they also felt that what they had was probably as good as it got.

This melancholy absence of faith in the transformative power of revolutionary politics is captured perfectly in Michael Powell's film version of *They're a Weird Mob*, where a shot of a hammer and sickle thrown idly on the ground at the building site cross-dissolves into an image of washing billowing in the breeze on a Hills hoist in the backyard next door. This was quite a perceptive touch on Powell's part given that he'd only been in the country a few weeks. But then, perhaps it was just so bloody obvious.

Such a widespread absence of a defined politics of existence left a space that was filled, in part, by the ideology of the self-made man. Not an ideology in the traditional, formalised sense of the term – a series of procedural tenets delineating a commitment to a politicised point of view – but rather a looser, more informal set of arrangements acting as a set of *organising categories for daily life*. This is basically what Nino is making a contribution to in *They're a Weird Mob*: giving us an intimate and detailed account of his self-transformation from the figure of a European who *writes*, into the character of an Australian who *builds*, laying a few more bricks and leaving a little more Old World intellectual baggage behind with each turn of the

37

page. This was a relatively easy move for O'Grady, because in the Australia of the self-made man the traditional hierarchies and class antagonisms that had played such a crucial role in the development of twentieth-century European political consciousness did appear, at first glance, to have been left behind. Witness Nino's observations of the relationship between Joe and Pat, the employee with whom Nino works on his first day: 'Joe was the boss, but Pat was no servant. Could it be that in Australia there were no masters and servants as we knew them?'[33]

An observation such as this circumscribes perfectly the quasi-classless, apolitical utopia within which the novel's action takes place. Apart from Pat's wry observation when Joe leaves Nino with him on his first day, that even 'Mr Menzies' would be a more competent and useful assistant, the text elides all references to the mainstream Australian politics of the period. And yet this was a time of great political upheaval in Australia, with the Cold War growing in intensity, with reds under beds, and with the Australian Labor Party (ALP) being torn apart in a fervent ideological and sectarian struggle. The Labor split was of particular concern to Australians of Irish ethnicity like O'Grady's fictional characters, with the formation of the anti-communist Democratic Labor Party (DLP) taking place in the same year in which *They're a Weird Mob* was published. Yet there is no real trace of the machinations of organised political life in the pages of the book. Its narrative operates on another level altogether, ignoring such surface struggles of public affairs in favour of an embrace of what was perhaps the quintessential myth of postwar Australia: that of the classless society, within which all participants were ultimately equal. Or, as a man who befriends Nino in the bar of a Kings Cross hotel tells him on his first afternoon in the country in response to his querying the unfamiliar word 'bloke': 'Oh, everybody's a bloke. You're a bloke. I'm a bloke. We're all blokes.'[34]

Except, of course, the fifty percent of the nation who were women, an omission dealt with quite beautifully in the film version: Powell repeats this scene almost word for word, but cuts this particular piece of dialogue over the top a shot of a silent, skeptical-looking woman working behind the bar. At the same time though, such complexities of gender and class and even ethnicity are exactly what the literary version of *They're a Weird Mob* is dedicated to effacing, with the ethic of building and developing, of simply getting on with the job at hand, ultimately dominating and even obliterating all such troublesome distractions.

It is the activities of this self-made man, what he builds, how he amuses himself in his spare time, rather than the politics of his existence that provides the central focus of the narrative of *They're a Weird Mob*. But to an important extent the self-made man's physical manifestation, his actual body, also plays a role. For example, Nino describes his new mate Pat in the following fashion:

> He commenced digging between the strings, the butt of his cigarette hanging from his lower lip. He was burnt nearly black by the sun, and I stood behind him admiring the play of muscles on his lean back. He wielded the heavy mattock effortlessly, moving his feet forward only when necessary, without breaking the rhythm of his steady strokes.[35]

This is a classically hard body – lean, muscular, suntanned – and a description that could simply be read as an exercise in homoerotica were it not for the frequent appearances of this trope in Australian writing, both fiction and journalism, of the period. For example, in a collection of essays published in 1953 titled *The Australian Way of Life*, the former diplomat and public intellectual Fredrick Eggleston described the situation thus: 'Physical activity has created an admiration for physical beauty which is truly Greek. A parade of lifesaving clubs on an Australian beach will provide a display of physical beauty which it would be difficult to match anywhere in the world.'[36] Even though they guzzle down beer as if it were water and gobble up steak and potatoes and fish and chips as if there were no tomorrow, Joe and the boys manage to stay true to this well-established healthy masculine ideal, mainly due to their vigour and tenacity in relation to the ongoing battle against empty blocks of land and piles of unlaid bricks. Inheriting in a very watered-down fashion certain features of twentieth-century English fiction (particularly, but not exclusively, that of D.H. Lawrence) in which the virile, heterosexual male body was idealised, O'Grady too writes of the physicality of his masculine workers in genuinely admiring terms.

This idealising of the working-class male body was also in keeping with a trend evident in Australian fiction over the previous few decades. Australian communist writers, women maybe even more so than men, had been writing about male bodies in this way since the 1930s. Jean Devanney's *Sugar Heaven* (1936) and *Cindie* (1949), filled as they are with glowing descriptions of the 'powerful limbs' of their working-class heroes, stand as excellent examples here. Arguably, such descriptions reached a climax with Dorothy Hewett's brilliant *Bobbin Up*, published the year after *They're a Weird Mob*, in 1958. There, for instance, as mill worker Jessie journeys home on a suburban train, she observes 'smoke-blackened loco sheds, steam trains gleaming and panting in the yards, a cleaner with a black face and a glistening, sweaty, beautiful body whistling to the girls hanging out the windows'.[37] In a couple of lines Hewett manages to eroticise not just her characters but even the industrial landscape they inhabit.

Compared to the audacity of Hewett's forcefully sensual description of her railway worker, O'Grady's depictions are rather timid. If this was partly owing to the enormous cultural gulf that separated the affable, middle-aged male chronicler of suburban bricklaying from the idealistic young female communist, it was also due to another, very significant factor. For while the physical attributes of his characters were important to O'Grady, they are in the end not his central focus. That's because he's ultimately less concerned with what his characters look like than with what they say.

They're a Weird Mob's narrative is rendered almost entirely in dialogue, and in an aggressively colloquial form of dialogue at that. O'Grady had quite specific reasons for choosing to write in this way. As he has Nino testify in the first few pages, 'in general, the conversations people have with each other cannot be reproduced in another language'. Subsequently, much of the narrative emerges through Nino's attempts to come to terms with Australian English:

> Now that I have got the hang of it, I want to write about it, and since it cannot be translated into any other language, including English, all I can do is put it down as I have heard it. To do this, I must put down also something about the people who speak it, and the situations where I heard it spoken. The troubles I had with it, too, must be described, so that Australians who read this book may realise how difficult it is for the foreigner, who has learned good English from books, to understand what the blazes they are yapping about![38]

Despite the fact that this is supposedly just an exercise in simple populist storytelling, there is a key theoretical premise underlining this passage: namely, the idea that language is always a social and cultural object. As Nino observes, in order to talk about the language of a people, one must also talk about the people in question, and their situation. On the one hand, O'Grady's purpose here is to depict the utter uniqueness of everyday Australian life by using the form of 'conversations people have with each other', something that 'cannot be translated into any other language'. And on the other hand, it is to make Australians aware of this perceived uniqueness, not just in terms of the world at large, but in relation to the foreigners in their midst. Because by the time of *They're a Weird Mob*, Australia had undergone a decade of massive immigration, both from Britain and more significantly from northern and southern Europe. In terms of the creation of a context for John O'Grady's work, the social and cultural consequences of this demographic redesign of Australia were crucial. For the first time in which any Australian alive could remember, the blanket cultural dominance of Anglos and Celts was being confronted on its own turf by new and different ways of being.

The great governmental paradox for Australia in the 1940s and 1950s was that if it was to survive as a discreet entity independent of the rest of the world, it could no longer hold the world outside its borders. Labor Immigration Minister Arthur Calwell's plan, continued by the Liberal-Country Party coalition after it won government at the end of 1949, was to bring as many 'New Australians' to the country as possible, ideally from Britain and Ireland. Such, though, was Australia's need, in Calwell's words, to 'populate or perish' that he and his department were forced to make up the shortfall in British immigrants by turning to the refugee camps of north Germany and their population of 'displaced persons' from Estonia, Latvia, Lithuania and East Prussia. Ethnicity remained the key criterion, however. In fact, so narrow were the racial categories from which these non-English-speaking immigrants were selected, even former members of the Nazi SS could qualify as New Australians provided they kept fairly quiet about their past. Yet it soon became obvious that not even this flow of 'Balts', as they were called, would be enough on its own to prevent Australia from perishing rather than populating. So in the late 1940s the New Australian category was expanded again, this time to include supposedly 'dark-skinned' peasants from southern Europe. As one woman from Trieste who applied to come to Australia in 1956 recalled, one of the best things about the Australian Government's screening process for prospective migrants was that it 'made you proud to be white.'[39]

This is the Australia that *They're a Weird Mob* speaks to, a nation whose governing classes were engaged in remaking the actual human substance of the nation in such a way that it didn't substantially differ from the form that already existed. This was a definitive act of social engineering underpinned by well-established twentieth century governmental principles and practices. Yet it was intended purely as a form of social rather than cultural engineering: the nation would absorb the bodies of the masses of new people it required, but not their ways of being in the world. As new subjects of a new nation, it was anticipated that the postwar immigrants would leave their old identities behind in their old countries.

Between 1947 and 1951 an average of 17,000 Italians migrated to Australia each year.[40] Yet the racialised climate of resistance to southern Europeans that had led Calwell and the Department of Immigration to seek out northern and eastern Europeans as preferred migrants in the first place was given voice in a range of organs both forming and amplifying conservative public opinion in Australia, from the editorials of the *Age* newspaper to *Reveille,* the journal of the New South Wales Branch of the Returned Services League (RSL). Italians, it was suggested, wouldn't make good Australians, with explanations ranging from the assertion that they were all communists, to the fear that they were all gangsters armed with flick knives, to observations that their performance in the recently concluded war had been 'despicable and deplorable'. The RSL even went so far as to suggest that former soldiers of the German Afrika Korps would make better immigrants than 'some of those who have come here from the Mediterranean ports'.[41]

By the late 1950s, though, such conservative opposition to the Italian presence in Australia had begun to soften, and to O'Grady's credit he set out to produce a text designed to soften such opinions even further. O'Grady presented Nino Culotta as the very ideal of the postwar migrant: he is the New Australian who will eventually *become Australian*. And this is a task for which Nino proves well suited, because, despite the fact that he is from southern Europe, he is no peasant. He is a middle-class journalist from Milan, a sophisticated northern Italian with a travelling trunk full of cultural capital that he can exchange for the affectations of an Aussie. In addition, Nino is tall and fair ('a big bloke' as the Australians he meets frequently observe), not some illiterate, undernourished agrarian worker, and this is a distinction O'Grady is constantly at pains to make. In fact, Nino looks down his nose at southern Italians the way narrow-minded Australians look down at him. In this way O'Grady uses a mechanism of displacement to open a sympathetic space for Nino in the intertwined hierarchy of race and class that existed in 1950s Australia.

At one point Nino even intervenes in a dispute on a suburban train between a verbally aggressive drunken Anglo-Australian and a sober, knife-wielding Sicilian, relieving the latter of his knife, throwing it from the carriage window, and then punching him unconscious, along with the drunk. In the parlance of the Australians for whom the book is supposedly written, this is clearly having a bob each way. And yet, as a narrative device, it works in terms of resetting the boundaries surrounding the central character, as it is an act that excludes both the European peasant and the Anglo drunk in favour of the category of *decent citizen*, a category capable of including a range of ethnicities united not by origins but by actions.

Or, to take another example, as Nino's self-employed builder boss, Joe, instructs Pat when he leaves Nino with him for his first day of work: 'Give 'im a go, mate . . . 'e'll be orright'.[42] This was the reality of populate or perish: if the nation were to survive the trauma of the massive influx of foreigners then the newcomers, initially at least, would have to be given a fair go. Subsequently, Nino finds that if he has a go then he'll be given a go, and that it really is that simple.

In *How to Do Things With Words*, J.L. Austin argues that the key aspect of language is its performative capacity. Rather than simply representing the world 'as it is', words possess a power generative of social action; in other words, they literally make things happen. In Austin's well-known example, the statement 'I bet you sixpence it will rain tomorrow' isn't a description of a situation, it is an act (or at least it was when sixpences existed) that initiates an action.[43]

And this is a social fact that the Australian experience impresses upon Nino Culotta, journalist as he is and so familiar with the power of words, almost immediately upon his arrival. 'Kings Bloody Cross', answers a surly cab driver when asked by Nino the name of the place where he is being dropped off.[44] Later on, while temporarily lost in the city streets, he has the following exchange with a policeman:

'Where do you live?' 'Kings Bloody Cross.'

'Keep using that language and you'll go to Central all right. Into a cell.'

'How can my language make me go to Central? It is good English language.'

'Are you fair dinkum.' 'No. I am Italian.'[45]

In the 1950s Central, conversational shorthand for the area around Central Station, was the location of the main police lockup in Sydney. With this example, as with many others, Nino finds that in Australia (as for all immigrants everywhere) the gap between words and things can often be an unfathomable chasm. On an existential level, Nino's problem in the conversation quoted above is that he is both Italian *and* fair dinkum, yet, until he masters this peculiar new system of signification within which he is now immersed, these two identities will remain mutually exclusive. Austin's point about the productive power of words is perfectly illustrated by this vignette. Via this exchange, Nino has been shown in the starkest terms possible that his improper use of the colloquial literally has the power to take him to a place he has absolutely no desire to go.

Through encounters such as this, Nino learns quite quickly that it is words as much as deeds that are crucial to the process of becoming

Australian. Not only do words possess the power to affect his physical position, they also possess the transformative power to reshape his identity. By the end of his first day's work he has successfully begun the process of cultural transformation to which the book is a testament. This isn't so much because he has demonstrated that he can stand in the hot sun for hours digging trenches at the building site (even though this is a crucial demonstration of manliness and 'Australian-ness'), but because he is sharp enough to pick up and then put to use the linguistic tools he hears in action around him. On entering a pub for an after work drink with his new mates, and asked by Joe what he will have, Nino answers: 'I reckon I could knock over a schooner'. The response is good-natured laughter all round, and Nino realises in an instant that, as far as his workmates are concerned, he has been 'accepted into their company'.[46]

From the point of view of cultural history, we could say that the stress O'Grady places in *They're a Weird Mob* on the value of the Australian way of speaking embodies the discourse of assimilation at the time, in both its official and unofficial forms. By the late 1950s the expansion of the immigration program had pushed the old order of White Australia (founded along with the nation in 1901) beyond its structural limits. In 1958 Commonwealth officers stopped administering the dictation test which had been the policy's fundamental tool of restriction since its inception. Within another decade or so, the entire White Australia policy itself had been quietly retired as Australia's official immigration strategy.

From the time European colonists began to take the landmass of Australia from its Indigenous owners until the middle of the twentieth century, the modern Australian nation had possessed a dominant form of racial coherence. Despite the presence of people from Asian and Pacific Island backgrounds, the great majority of the population was still British and White, and it could logically be defended on the basis of 'correct' and 'incorrect' racial types. However, once the dominant notion of race began to be compromised by an ever-increasing expansion of the category of White to include southern Europeans, language was forced to carry ever more of the burden of defining the preferred national type. Similarly, as the defining category of race (White) tied to language (English) became more and more unworkable as an administrative technology, so the cultural concept 'way of life' became increasingly crucial as a delineating marker. This is why O'Grady has Nino testify that he can't record the Australian language without also providing a record of the people who speak it, because, in a society no longer defined on the basis of racial homogeneity, way of life is now *the* indicator of what constitutes an Australian. And this way of life, in turn, is only really made palpable via constant articulation – performance – of the language that constitutes it.

In 1957 *They're a Weird Mob* was therefore launched into circulation in a nation that, for the previous six decades, had its racial and cultural integrity defended by a dictation test. Now though, discrimination on the basis of language (as a default category for race) was no longer official policy, rather it had been replaced by the idea of assimilation, an apparently organic governmental response to the increasing numbers of foreigners within the borders of the nation. There was now no question that Australia needed to accept foreigners, but it was very much a reciprocal arrangement. As far as the opinion makers and policy planners were concerned, the foreigners who were invited in would need just as much to accept Australia.

Much of the discursive force of assimilation, as it is manifested in *They're a Weird Mob*, works through a choice of words as markers for a way of being in the world. Australian words, it would seem, really do have the power to make their speaker 'Australian'. And this, ultimately, is the message that Nino, pseudo-Italian-Anglo-Celtic-Australian, imparts to his readers. As he advises New Australians towards the end of his narrative: 'Mix with Australians, listen to them, work with them, and practise in secret the sentences you hear, so that you can say them exactly as you heard them.'[47]

It is difficult not to draw the conclusion from passages such as this that O'Grady was being at least a little ironic in his celebration of the virtues of the Australian way of life. Again, he seems to have been backing more than one horse in this particular race, as the following stridently assimilationist statement from the book's conclusion attests:

> There are far too many New Australians in this country who are still mentally living in their homelands, who mix with people of their own nationality, and try to retain their own language and customs. Who even try to persuade Australians to adopt their customs and manners. Cut it out. There is no better way of life in the world than that of the Australian. I firmly believe this . . . He fears no one, crawls to no one, and acknowledges no master. Learn his way. Learn his language.[48]

Had *They're a Weird Mob* been a novel of little impact, an obscure piece of working class fiction that had sold only moderately, its significance as an object of culture would be principally as a curio. It was, however, anything but obscure. In fact, it was probably the most widely read, or at least widely disseminated, work of fiction ever published in Australia. Yet in relentlessly adhering to only one perspective in its account of the Italian-Australian immigrant experience of the 1950s, and presenting this as a definitive account, and indeed amplifying this claim by purporting to speak with the voice of an actual immigrant, *They're a Weird Mob* embodied an aggressively one-sided narrative of the migrant experience. And within the climate of 1950s assimilationist Australia no real-life Italian immigrant was likely to come forward to present an alternative version of the story to Nino Culotta's, as neither Australia's publishing industry, nor the overwhelmingly Anglo-Celtic reading public, could have supported such an author even if one had existed. It would be more than two decades before an Italian-Australian author produced such a book, *Paese fortunato* (1981) – *Oh Lucky Country* (1984) – and inevitably, perhaps, in terms of the major transformations of the cultural landscape over this time, the author would be a woman, Rosa Cappiello.

At the peak of its phenomenal popularity, the closest approximation in textual form to any kind of counter argument to the assimilationist preaching of *They're a Weird Mob* appeared not in Australia but in Italy, and not in the form of a work of popular fiction, but in a single scene of a European art film. The narrative of Michelangelo Antonioni's masterpiece of 1959, *L'Avventura*, follows a group of friends as they search the coastal islands and towns of northern Sicily for a member of their party who has gone missing from a boating holiday. On a small and barren island, with night coming on and a storm approaching, they take shelter in a hut. Soon the occupant appears, a fisherman, who tells the three bourgeois Romans about how he has come back to the island after thirty years living in Australia. But these narcissists have no interest in his story: they ask him no questions about himself, or Australia, or the years he spent there; all they care about is the adventure of their search. Indeed the film's macho protagonist, Sandro, goes on to push the peasant around in the very same way that Nino pushes around the southern Italian he meets on the train in *They're a Weird Mob*.

Following the brief encounter with the fisherman, the narrative of *L'Avventura* moves on to mainland Sicily, leaving him on his island. We don't see him again and we learn no more about him. Yet this nameless peasant is an infinitely more authentic migrant figure than O'Grady's fictional Nino, with all his exploitative humour. One of the hallmarks of Italian Neo-Realist cinema, of which Antonioni was one of the pioneers, was the use of non-professional actors in lesser roles, and this unnamed man from the Aeolian Islands is more than likely telling his own rather than an invented story. He'd travelled halfway across the world, struggled and got by and, even though he speaks nostalgically of his years in Australia, for some reason things there didn't work out, so he returned to his Mediterranean home. Clearly, this ex-migrant didn't follow O'Grady's orders to 'learn the way' of the Australian in order to 'get accepted by him', and thereby never leave the Promised Land.

Antonioni's fisherman wasn't alone in having his migration journey end up back where it started. In 1961 the Italian government suspended its bilateral migration treaty with Australia, which had been in place for the previous decade, on the grounds that Italian emigrants weren't receiving as good a deal in relation to assisted passage and access to welfare as were the 'favoured' migrants of northern Europe and Britain. Consequently, over the next few years ever-greater numbers of Italians began to return home from Australia while fewer chose to make the trip out. In 1967, however, a new treaty was negotiated addressing the key issues in the Italians' favour, and emigration numbers began to rise again.[49]

Given this context, the fisherman's story stands in direct contrast to that of Nino Culotta. Yet it is also limited as a retort to O'Grady's appropriation of an Italian speaking position. While this brief moment in *L'Avventura* provides an authentic voice to speak back to that of the exceedingly inauthentic Nino Culotta, it does so in a textual context that is quite dissimilar to that of a populist novel, because it is an art film and so, by its very nature, a profoundly bourgeois text. Subtitled and released into Australian cinemas in the early 1960s as an archetype of the foreign film, the Cannes Film Festival Jury Prize-winning *L'Avventura* was screening to Anglo-Australians at the very same time that the nation was reading *Cop This Lot* (1960), O'Grady's sequel to *They're a Weird Mob*, but it is highly unlikely that the two texts found much common ground in terms of an audience.

The modernist text, both literary and cinematic, often contained an element of direct social and or cultural critique, but in liberal capitalist democracies this has generally been a form of critique tailored to an audience possessed of enough cultural capital both to make sense of it and to desire it in the first place. As O'Grady famously said, Patrick White's *Voss* was a work he just 'couldn't understand'.[50] Similarly, even with subtitles, *L'Avventura* was still speaking a language unfamiliar to the majority of Australian fans of the populist O'Grady. Perhaps this is an inevitable consequence of the fact that a popular text will tend to be ideologically complacent: in order to achieve and maintain popularity it will always need to be in harmony with the status quo, hence the ongoing role of the avant-garde within the social and cultural experiences of modernity as an elitist, anti-popular force.

While O'Grady as Nino Culotta usurped the Italian migrant 'voice' for his mainly Anglo-Australian readers, this didn't mean that competing voices were wholly absent from the circuits of local popular culture. They were just not speaking English, but Italian, and, in one instance, Calabrian dialect.[51] Salvatore Tripodi migrated from Palmi in Calabria to Melbourne in 1952, but didn't enjoy the experience and returned home after a few years. Working in the oral story-telling tradition of the *Cantastorie*, Tripodi recounted how the desire for economic advancement lured him to Australia and into a menial job in a suburban Melbourne glass factory. Yet despite the hype, all Australia seemed to offer the migrant was material well-being, and ultimately, for Tripodi, these economic advantages were of little consequence when compared to the greater riches of the friendly social environment back at home, and the warmth and love of family.

Cantastorie, or ballad-singing narration, is a mixture of humorous songs and anecdotes, and *Le Avventure di Salvatore Tripodi* found material form as a 45rpm record that circulated amongst Italians, particularly Calabrians, living in Melbourne and Sydney in the early 1960s. In a mixture of Italian, Calabrian and Australian English, Tripodi offered the sort of advice to his listeners that would have seen O'Grady and Nino Culotta fuelling their barbecues with his record: don't be tricked into thinking Australia was 'the land of milk and honey. Stay in your own homes and enjoy life with your little ones'. Subsequently, Tripodi recorded further oral accounts of his Australian adventures for a Palmi record company, recordings that were still selling in the early twenty first century.[52]

Tripodi's satirising of the Italian-Australian economic migrant experience was very much in the long tradition of Southern Italian cultural mockery, exemplified perhaps by the translation of Goethe's iconic *Die Leiden von Junges Werther* into a Neapolitan puppet show in the early nineteenth century.[53] In this sense Tripodi's work formed an ideal counterpoint to O'Grady's Weird Mob, but it is important to note that this was oral storytelling, not prose fiction, and that even within the dynamics of the era's popular culture there were still strict delineations and boundaries as regards access to texts. O'Grady was writing for an audience that read English and was acutely sensitive to the nuances of written representations of their language, while Tripodi was recording for an audience that spoke both broader Italian and Calabrian dialect. Given the ethno-cultural dynamics of Australia at the time, these two groups were, largely, mutually exclusive, despite the presence of crossover figures like O'Grady's fictional Nino. Generally, New Australians knew all about *They're a Weird Mob*, but they also knew that it was a book about them, not for them. Meanwhile, the average Anglo-Australian didn't even have a clue that Salvatore Tripodi existed.

They're a Weird Mob is often credited with leading Anglo-Australians to an acceptance of New Australians, but while O'Grady's work may have played some role in this development, it is far too narrow a text to deserve unqualified acclaim. Immigration succeeded and Australia grew and prospered not because of a patronising, conservative work of popular fiction by an imposter writer, but because of the countless personal struggles waged every day over decades by hundreds of thousands of nameless immigrants, the true heroes of postwar Australia: people like the fisherman in *L'Avventura*, the people who worked hard and built a complex multicultural nation, in which respect for difference displaced the dead hand of assimilation.

Initially, the example of *They're a Weird Mob* leaves one in little doubt as to why conservative politicians like John Howard and Pauline Hanson spent the late 1990s expressing the desire to 'take Australia back to the 1950s'. The simplistic, assimilationist landscape sketched out as the background to the antics of Nino Culotta really does depict a conservative utopia. The book's final two sentences see O'Grady's two-handed irony in full flight, with Nino thanking God for letting him be an Australian, and then speculating that perhaps God is in fact an Australian Himself.[54] Accept these New Australians, O'Grady seems to be saying, but don't accept them for what they are. Accept them if, and only if, they are prepared to become 'like us'. In terms of both style and content this message differs not at all from that trumpeted by John Howard forty years later. This is quite paradoxical, because it is precisely to this period of great cultural uncertainty, of a massive twisting of the fabric of the nation and of struggle and debate over what it was that truly made 'an Australian', that Howard and Hanson and their like dream of 'returning'.

But it never really was the way the dream would have us believe. The supposed golden years of the 1950s actually constitute the period in which it became clear once and for all that the world was never going to 'leave Australia alone', and that the country could never just shut the door and hope that the rest of humanity would go away, even if this had been the guiding dream of Federation some fifty years earlier. Indeed, it was at this time that so many of the key decisions were made which have produced our contemporary globalised nation, with the decision to open up Australia to a diverse population from all over the world being perhaps the most important of them all.

Rather, if there is something truly significant about *They're a Weird Mob*, it is its rendering of the speech of Anglo-Celtic working-class Australians. It is remarkable that O'Grady manages to both capture and reproduce a genuinely oral idiom in a way that allows it to live and breathe, rather than blurring or reducing it. However, this too serves ends that are ultimately quite conservative. The characters may work and strive, but they do so within a purely market-driven society: there are no trade unions, no government services, no tax officials; indeed, other than cops, there are no organs of civil society of any kind present within the pages of the book. Again this is a remarkably selective rendering of the times, all the more so for the fact that, as previously noted, it was written in the decade in which Menzies tried to eliminate communism from Australian's political canvas, and the Australian Labor Party split apart over the very same issue.

John O'Grady claimed that he wasn't really a writer of fiction, but a social commentator, and that his work was in essence 'reporting with exaggeration'.[55] In the end though, the key point is that *They're a Weird Mob* isn't an exercise in social commentary but an intensely ideological work of fiction. And, in this sense, it really is an exercise in persuasion: in persuading 'Old' Australians that they should relax their xenophobia to some degree and accept the New Australians, provided, of course, that the New Australian is worthy of being accepted, a judgment that in the last instance will always rest on the degree to which the foreigner in question is prepared to assimilate.

To a great extent John O'Grady's astoundingly popular book was a cultural tool to help Anglo-Celtic Australians deal with this self-initiated invasion of the foreign. And this really is the crucial element that permitted the book to speak to such a massive audience. If the national subject hadn't been undergoing such a severe identity crisis as that provoked by the postwar immigration program, then this particular text would never even have needed to exist. Essentially, *They're a Weird Mob* is a guide to being an assimilated Australian, and in many ways it was simply a lifestyle book, one that was a bestseller in an era before the lifestyle book had even been invented.

4. The Taj Mahal

For most Australians in the early 1960s, trees were not considered a subject worthy of impassioned political debate. In this period, at the peak of the postwar boom, the arboreal state of the nation didn't represent a potential vote-catcher for Australian politicians. Nor did the issue present any kind of ethical conundrum for the average Australian. Trees, if they were thought about at all, were usually viewed as annoying objects which needed to be removed so that some worthwhile activity could occur or some useful structure be built in their place. After all, there were lots of them out there.

So when a combined Army and Federal Department of Supply team set off the most powerful non-nuclear explosion ever seen in Australia at Cape York one morning in July 1963, there were no protests, no outraged greenies, no questions in parliament. Australians were used to explosions. Throughout the 1950s the national newspapers had carried images of mushroom clouds over Maralinga and the Monte Bello Islands, as Australia played its supporting role in both the Cold War and Britain's increasingly desperate attempts to prove it could still match it with the superpowers on the international stage.[56] Obediently, the *Sydney Morning Herald* reported Australia's own big explosion, 'Operation Blowdown', in glowing terms, under the headline 'A-Bomb Rocks Jungle in Army's Cape York Test'. Technically it was really only 'a' bomb, not an actual A-Bomb, but still, it showed that if we tried we could be just as purposefully destructive as anyone else: 'the biggest conventional explosion ever set off in Australia today flattened a huge area of jungle near the tip of the Cape York peninsula', announced the *Herald*.[57]

There was to this explosion much more of a point than just the performative or demonstrative. It was an actual experiment in devastation, and a successful one at that. Ernest Titterton, Professor of Nuclear Physics at the Australian National University and a man in thrall to the iconic power of the atom, observed that while there may have been 'less light output than in an atomic explosion . . . the shock waves moved quite nicely across the jungle canopy'. The newspaper story went on to detail how steel-shielded cameras recorded in slow motion the disintegration of trees painted in various colours. Experts are studying the scatter of coloured splinters to calculate the damage a nuclear explosion would cause in jungle country. They are also studying the effects of the blast on dummy soldiers and dumps of food and equipment.[58]

There were seventy official observers present at the explosion: a collection of Australian Army officers, scientists and public servants, along with others from Britain and Australia's ANZUS allies, the United States and New Zealand. After the dust had settled they entered the wasteland and inspected the effects of their blast: the explosion had given them what they wanted, there were coloured splinters everywhere. One American observer even found an artificial leg complete with boot and military gaiter, and held it up for the photographers. It was all that was left of a dummy soldier that had been placed in the jungle near ground zero.

This event seems a long time ago now, a minor incident from a time in the life of the nation that has slipped into history and popular memory: Australia in the Cold War. But the military and political struggles that had produced this ersatz nuclear test on behalf of Australia were real enough. In England, the self-exiled American

Stanley Kubrick had just finished his film *Dr Strangelove or: How I Learned to Stop Worrying and Love the Bomb*, which closes with Vera Lynne singing *We'll Meet Again* as a nuclear holocaust swallows up the earth. In America JFK, who would be dead within six months, was trying to work out how to get his 16,000 military 'advisers' out of South Vietnam without being seen as 'soft on communism'. In Saigon, Buddhist monks were setting themselves alight in protest at their oppression by the Catholic-dominated, US-sponsored dictatorship of President Diem. In the Soviet Union Nikita Khruschev, who had lost the most recent round of the global struggle, his attempt to put nuclear-armed missiles in Cuba, was in the last year of his reign.[59] And in Australia, the Menzies Government was negotiating to buy F-111 bombers from the Americans so that Australia could, if our already fraught relations with Indonesia turned openly hostile, attack Jakarta.

The modern world was an uncertain, precarious place, war was a constant possibility, and annihilation seemed just around the corner. This was what the mannequin's severed leg, held up by the American in the ruined Cape York jungle, said to Australians. It was a warning that unless they stood firm with each other as much as with their allies, unless they held together in the face of their enemies, then the much-envied freedom of this ever so lucky country would be taken away, and their way of life blown to pieces, just like the body of the imaginary soldier. What price then was the destruction of a small patch of jungle in the playing of such a high stakes game? We had already sacrificed the Monte Bello Islands off the north coast of Western Australia and the desert scrub around Maralinga in South Australia, sacrificed them to the testing of Britain's nuclear arsenal, sacrificed them to the march of science, sacrificed them to the defence of the West, the defence of what used to be called the Empire, the defence of a White Australia, and so on. It was a big country, and we could go on sacrificing parts of it, back of beyond, as long as was necessary. A patch of scrub up north, who would miss it?

And, anyway, from such destruction came progress. This was the spiritual basis of modernity, a set of ethics that in many ways incorporated the spirit of Australia. As we know, modernity was dedicated to the constant remaking of itself, the constant extension of a perpetually unsatisfied present into a continuously improving future. Australia as both a nation and an idea grew from just such experiential and philosophic soil. Wherever the white man went after 1788 it was to destroy in order to create: to dig and excavate, to carve and channel, to burn, to build upon, to destroy, and to begin again. This was the national project that was Australia. And while nothing would actually be built in the space cleared by the big bang at Cape York, it was an act of progress all the same. For, from the blasted trees and the mangled bush would arise facts and figures on desolation and ruin, and from such facts and figures would Australia's soldiers and scientists grow just that much more aware of the damage we could do, and that could be done to us.

There were no complaints about this wanton act of destruction, because there was no one to speak on behalf of the ravaged bush. Australian politics in those days was, as it had been for a century, still largely a struggle between white men over how to best carve up the national pie. Whether or not the bosses would get all the big pieces, or whether they would be forced to share some with the workers: this was the key to Australian politics. Concern for the rights of Indigenous Australians and for the state of the environment were issues awaiting the middle-class counter-culture revolution that would sweep across the West in the next decade, entrenching these causes as legitimate political concerns. Of course the part of Cape York that the Army chose to blow up had its traditional owners, but they weren't consulted. Nor, in 1963, were they in the position to speak to the nation about the fate of their land, to which they didn't even possess any form of legal title. They were bound to silence by the state bureaucracy that had regulated their lives since the nineteenth century.

*

The visible face of Australian political life at this time wasn't the struggle for Aboriginal rights, it was the struggle of the Cold War. Later in 1963 Menzies would call an early election in order to exploit the divisions opened up by the ongoing global contest. At the previous federal election in 1961, the Liberal-Country Party coalition had held on to government by one seat in Brisbane, and even this was only retained thanks to DLP and Communist Party preferences. The next year, Menzies announced that a communications centre for American submarines would be constructed at North West Cape, on the north coast of Western Australia. This base would direct America's nuclear submarines. As a result, Australia would now be a nuclear target.

We like to think of wedge politics as a recent phenomenon, as a product of the cynicism of the Howard Government (1996–2007). In reality, wedge politics has been around for as long as parliamentary democracy, dependent as it is on the one environment in which it really thrives: the class system. One absolute master of the technique was Howard's hero, Robert Menzies, and in the early 1960s questions of how far to go in an alliance with the nuclear-armed United States were, despite their crucial strategic nature, also perfect devices with which to 'wedge' the Labor Party.

Naturally, Labor was divided over how to respond to North West Cape. The Left faction wanted to reject the base outright while the Right wanted to accommodate it. At a special meeting of the Federal Conference of the ALP in Canberra in March 1963 the party's leadership, Arthur Calwell (Left) and Gough Whitlam (Right), came up with a compromise by convincing the delegates from the various states to accept the base as a joint facility run by both the Australian and the American military. In those days the party leadership had no actual voice on the floor of the conference, so, when it came time after midnight to vote on the proposal, Calwell and Whitlam were actually standing on the footpath outside the conference venue, the Hotel Kingston, waiting for the outcome. As it turned out, the Federal Executive accepted their proposition by just one vote.

Alan Reid, journalist, raconteur, political stirrer and Sir Frank Packer's 'agent in Canberra', saw them standing there.[60] He also saw someone else he knew leaving the public bar, a man he'd met through a shared interest in trout fishing. Reid knew that this amateur fisherman was also an amateur photographer, and he asked him to go home, get his camera and flashbulb and come back, which he did, and then he took a few photos of Calwell and Whitlam and sold them to Reid on the spot. This exchange proved to be far more important than anything that occurred inside the conference room because, according to next day's *Daily Telegraph* (an influential Packer family mouthpiece), the photographs illustrated how the ALP was ruled: not by its elected representatives, but by 'thirty-six virtually unknown men'.[61] It was a killer of a line, and it would still be bedeviling the Labor Party well into the twenty first century.

In *Telegraph* articles, and backed by editorials, Alan Reid had been questioning Labor's foreign and defence policies for weeks leading up to the conference. 'Calwell Gives No Lead on Defence', 'ALP Crisis Looms', 'Rebuff to Calwell on Radio Base', were just some of the *Telegraph* headlines.[62] But it was this story on the Friday after the Federal Executive vote that really hit the target. Indeed, not only did it generate one of the most powerful epithets in Australian political history, it was also a key moment of transformation in the history of Australian political journalism. For the story took the form of a photo essay, a type of text pioneered two decades earlier by American publications like *Life* magazine. Now, for the first time in the telling of Australian politics, it was images rather than words that really carried the burden of representation.

Splashed across two pages of the newspaper were five black-and-white photographs of Arthur Calwell and Gough Whitlam 'waiting in the midnight darkness outside Canberra's Kingston Hotel'. Also present were Calwell's press secretary, Graham Freudenberg, and sundry conference delegates who had popped out from time to time to tell them what was going on. Most of those captured on film, apart from Calwell (at that time the recognisable face of Labor), were photographed back to camera, and their images ran in the paper under a headline reading: 'Waiting for Instructions . . . from Their Bosses – Leaders or Office Boys?'[63] Reid went on: 'The Conference has demonstrated that it regards the Federal Parliamentary Labor leader, not as an alternative Prime Minister, a leader and an adviser, but as lackey.' Menzies weighed in too: 'The people of Australia have had a sharp reminder that an Australian Labor government would not be responsible to the people or even to its own judgment.' Two days later the *Sunday Telegraph* provided a profile of 'the 36 who decide ALP policy' and 'tell Calwell what to do'.[64] Given the temper of the times Reid's dramatic conclusion was predictable enough: 'Close analysis of the numbers', he wrote, 'shows the alarming way the Communist Party has been able to manipulate the conference.'

Had the ALP really been a hotbed of communists, then the Kingston would have been a curious place for them to conduct their affairs, as it was located directly across the road from the Soviet embassy, and so was the principal observation post for the Australian Security Intelligence Office (ASIO) in its surveillance of the Russians in Canberra.[65] Nonetheless, Reid's alarmist imagery did its trick, and the pictures told the story required. Fifty years later Australian politics would be circumscribed first and foremost by image rather than analysis and by an accompanying rhetoric of superficiality. But this is where this particular aspect of the triumph of image over substance really began for Australian politics: outside the Hotel Kingston, in the quiet hours of a March night in 1963.

Befitting its prescience, Alan Reid's photojournalistic scoop worked its way into contemporary popular culture. Quickly, despite the fact that every last one of them had been named and profiled by Reid in his *Sunday Telegraph* story, Labor's 'anonymous' conference delegates became known as 'the 36 faceless men'. How, in such troubled times, could Australians entrust the leadership of their country to a group of faceless men, asked Menzies? During the election campaign nine months later the Coalition would run newspaper advertisements featuring the photographs and asking Australians who they would trust to govern Australia – Parliament, or 'the 36 faceless men'.[66]

As Gilles Deleuze and Félix Guattari put it in their landmark work *A Thousand Plateaus*, 'the face is a politics'.[67] Even though he was certainly no postmodern philosopher, Robert Menzies knew this too. A face gives coherence, a literal personification, to the dynamics and assemblages of power that concentrate at particular points within the social field. At this moment in Cold War Australia, Menzies' visage thrust itself forward as the face of the nation, the face that represented conservative guidance of the ship of state. Meanwhile, Labor now had no face. It had been exposed as faceless, just like the amorphous tyranny of communism, where decisions were always made behind closed doors, and orders were always carried out in the dark.

In fact totalitarian communism was even more facialised than liberal democracy, with absolute power radiating outwards from the radically overexposed faces of Lenin, Stalin and Mao, and even, in Menzies' heyday, from the grinning, gangsterish face of Khruschev.

But the counter-image of a faceless conspiracy of the left extending unbroken from Moscow to the Canberra headquarters of the Australian Labor Party made for a more effective politics of fear, and Menzies and his government played it for all it was worth. At the early election that Menzies called for November 1963, a week after Kennedy was shot, Labor lost ten seats. Later, the function room of the Hotel Kingston was renamed 'The 36 Faceless Men Lounge'.

In four years' time Labor would get its face back when Calwell retired and was replaced by Gough Whitlam, whose massive countenance would go on to adorn and eventually haunt the party for the foreseeable future. In terms of the machinations and practicalities of politics, Whitlam soon found the stigma of the 36 faceless men very useful in his own struggle to subdue the Left-dominated Victorian branch of the ALP and reorganise the party structures so that no more federal parliamentary leaders had to stand on footpaths while policy was decided without them.

In terms of the political sphere, what Alan Reid and Sir Frank Packer were demanding, using the hysteria beat up over the 36 faceless men, was that the ALP abolish this 'communist-like' practice of allowing party officials rather than parliamentarians to determine policy. Yet on another level they were also demanding something else much more significant. For it was the metaphor of the closed door as much as the faceless men that was central to the issue. It was not just that the ALP's appointed officials were working out policy, it was that they were doing it in a space to which the press had no access. Alan Reid was just as excluded as Calwell and Whitlam: he was out there on the footpath with them. And this, I suspect, pissed him off even more than any supposed affront to liberal democracy. So, in the cultural arena in which the day-to-day machinations of politics are actually played out, what the *Telegraph* was demanding was that such invisible processes as Labor's Federal Conference be dragged into the space of the mediasphere.

It was with images such as these, of the severed leg of a dummy soldier on Cape York, and the 36 faceless men at the Hotel Kingston in Canberra, that an increasingly powerful set of communication technologies shaped and articulated the nation's fears. In the case of these particular examples, an American military official held one up for examination, while a self-important journalist, a meddle-some media baron, and a conservative prime minister propagated the other. Such sources sketched in turn the complex currents of power running through the body of the nation. The message, though, was simple enough: Australians had to bond together or be blown apart. But their bonding must be that of one independent individual to another, not that of the undifferentiated mass or mob.

*

The day after the newspaper reports of the big blast, Saturday 20 July 1963, another event of social and cultural significance took place, this time in southern Sydney. This was a ceremony of significance for many of the 700,000 people living in the south and southwest of Australia's largest city, particularly working-class men of Anglo-Celtic background, because it was on this day that the St George Leagues Club officially opened at Kogarah, just across the Princes Highway from Kogarah Oval, the home ground of the St George District Rugby League Football Club. Costing A£750,000 to con-struct, the new club was described as the 'largest and one of the most luxurious sporting clubhouses in Sydney', a club destined to become both 'the most famous in all clubdom' and 'the hub of social life in the St George district'.[68] As the local newspaper the *St George Call* saw it, the building was 'one of the most modern of its kind in the

Southern Hemisphere', and its 'decor and appointments brought gasps of admiration from all'.[69]

As a cultural phenomenon, the St George Leagues Club's origin lay in the humble form of the sporting clubhouse, but in both style and content its closest cousin was the Las Vegas casino: all glitz, glamour and gambling, though without the window-dressing of roulette wheels and card tables as the club was, in essence, a venue for the playing of poker machines. In the early 1960s New South Wales enjoyed the most liberal gaming laws in Australia, and the licensed club industry was positively booming, like much of the nation now that the recession of 1961, which is what had brought the Menzies Government so close to losing office that year, was fading quickly from memory.

By 1963 in Australia, this land of perpetual boom and bust, to get rich was once again glorious. And for the twelve directors of the St George Leagues Club, as they basked in the reflected glory and congratulated themselves on the accomplishment of their task, there was much satisfaction to be gained from the fact that they had turned their passion for a beer after the playing of a particular code of football into such a money-spinning palace of dreams. All agreed that the singularly most impressive thing about the new club was its size. A few days after the opening the chairman of the New South Wales Rugby League, Bill Buckley, attended a dinner in the club's main dining room. As he walked through the foyer, so the story goes, the well-travelled Buckley 'looked around and declared "This reminds me very much of the Taj Mahal"'.[70] From that moment on the St George Leagues Club would be known colloquially as the Taj Mahal.

The St George club was only one of many leagues clubs throughout metropolitan and rural New South Wales. As part of his unique social history, *The Mighty Bears!*, Andrew Moore has traced the record of a similar institution, the North Sydney Leagues Club. Moore argues that as a specific form the leagues club had developed from two earlier club models: the Returned Services League clubs created after the First World War, and the workers' clubs of the industrial areas of Sydney, Newcastle and Wollongong, which had appeared around the same time. Subsequently, after the Second World War key legislative decisions by the New South Wales Parliament – ending the monopoly brewing companies enjoyed over the supply of their product in 1954, and passing the *Gaming and Betting (Poker Machines) Taxation Act* which regulated and facilitated the placement of the machines in registered clubs in 1956 – created a formal legal architecture within which the leagues clubs could flourish.

The egalitarian nature of the registered club, as opposed to the elitism of the gentlemen's club, to which the word *club* had referred prior to the 1920s, was crucial to both their function and identity. As Rex Connor, the state Labor member for Wollongong, said in parliament while defending poker machines and the income they provided for clubs: 'the club is the working man's castle, and in the industrial areas the trade unionist claims the right to go to his club, where he enjoys exactly the same privileges as are normally enjoyed in the city by only the privileged members of the community'.[71] Connor was a very public man. Robert Menzies may have been hell-bent on building a society in which a man was only truly happy in his own personal castle, his home, but for Connor the opposite was true: only the community could build a castle, not the individual. Connor never deviated from this belief and two decades later, as the Whitlam Government's Minister for Minerals and Energy, he would try to borrow four billion dollars from Saudi Arabia to build the ultimate public castle, his and Gough Whitlam's dream of a corporate, industrial state.

In postwar Australia clubs were springing up everywhere on the back of the pokies. They may have owed their foundations to one communitarian cause or another, but from wherever one sat or stood within those capacious walls, the ratchet of the metal arm, the clatter of the illuminated wheels, and the far too infrequent clanging of the jackpot bell were never far away. For example, North Sydney Leagues Club opened in 1955 specifically as 'a social venture aimed to assist the propagation of Rugby League in the North Sydney district', yet at the same time, the North Sydney officials had actually been prompted to create their club by the commercial success they'd observed during a visit to the St George premises in 1953.[72]

The first St George Leagues Club, on the corner of Rocky Point Road and the Princes Highway, had opened a few months earlier, initially with just two poker machines and, because of a brewery monopolists' embargo, selling beer obtained from two small breweries in Lithgow and Mudgee.[73] Right from the start it was a going concern. The war had been over for nearly a decade, and those few brief years in which Australians had been forced to pay the price of victory were fading too. Postwar prime minister Ben Chifley had been dead for two years, and gone with him were his socialism, his ration cards, his officious rules and regulations, and all the other paraphernalia of the undertaking that was 'the light on the hill'. Now there was a new kind of nation being built, and everywhere, or so it seemed, there were blokes with a thirst, a quid in their pocket, and a few idle hours to fill in after work before they went home to the missus. According to Glynn Price, the foundation treasurer, the St George Leagues Club made A£3,000 profit in its first six months.[74]

By the end of the 1950s the club's premises were far too small for the enterprise it had become, so Glynn Price, manager Arthur 'Snowy' Justice, and chairman Baden Wales, were all looking to further develop their business. It wasn't possible to expand on the site, nor was there any space for a car park. This was a crucial issue, for the suburbs of postwar Australia were, more than anything else, creations of the car industry. And nowhere was this better illustrated in the era of the self-made man than in the St George district. A railway line curved through the north of the district from Arncliffe to Hurstville, but it was to the south and east, along the Georges River and Botany Bay, that the quarter-acre blocks and their brick castles abounded.

The St George Rugby League Football Club had entered the Sydney competition in 1921.The club's first permanent ground was Earl Park, at Arncliffe, in the north of the district and on the edge of the inner city, where most of Sydney's other rugby league teams, like Glebe, Balmain, South Sydney and Newtown, were located. Football club meetings were held at the Arncliffe School of Arts hall a few streets away. But by 1940 Earl Park had become a valuable piece of inner urban land, and it was sold and redeveloped as an industrial site. The St George home ground then moved south, to Hurstville, for ten years. In 1950 St George settled permanently into Jubilee Oval at Kogarah, where it would remain until a merger with Illawarra some fifty years later saw half of each season's home games played in Wollongong. But, in the course of the 1940s and 1950s, the district's football focus, following one key trajectory of Sydney's postwar sub-urban sprawl, was Kogarah.

In the course of *The Mighty Bears!* Andrew Moore ponders the question of why the North Sydney Bears only ever won the Sydney Premiership twice, and consecutively at that, in 1921 and 1922. For Moore the answer is obvious. It was in the following year, 1923, that Britain's Dorman Long Construction Company and the New South Wales Public Works Department began building the Sydney Harbour Bridge and its adjacent road approaches, resulting in the 'decimation of the North Sydney district'. Five hundred cottages – the homes of a significant proportion of the area's working-class population – were demolished, their occupants dispersed to other parts of city. In one spectacular sweep of the hand of progress, rugby league, the 'working man's game', had lost a major segment of its support base in North

Sydney. Four decades later, in another burst of expansion of the urban transport infrastructure, the same thing happened again. Moore continues: 'In 1965 Billy Wilson and the Bears reached the final. Despite giving and taking a battering they failed to reach the grand final. In 1966 the construction of the Warringah Expressway completed the trauma that had begun in 1923.'[75] And from there on it was mostly downhill all the way to oblivion. There are no Bears anymore.

For St George it was a very different story. The district was a prime example of the postwar boom made manifest. It was filled with self-employed tradesman and small businessmen, men who were building the actual infrastructure of the suburban boom and presiding, in their domestic hours, over car-owning nuclear families. Such social strength and authority spilled over on to the football field, as it did into all areas of cultural life. For example, the Bears had failed to make it to the Grand Final in 1965 because they were beaten 47-7 in the final by St George, a team which, at this point, was on the biggest winning streak in football history having won the Sydney Premiership for the previous nine consecutive years. A week after beating Norths, the Saints would defeat South Sydney in the Grand Final and win the premiership again, in front of a crowd of 78,000 people squeezed, somehow, into the confines of the Sydney Cricket Ground, an arena intended to hold no more than about 50,000. The next year, 1966, St George would win the Grand Final once again, pushing out their record to eleven years in a row. Despite the fact that on a mercantile level the football club and the leagues club were separate commercial entities, the building of the Taj Mahal was very much a reflection of St George's relentless dominance of rugby league in Australia. More than just a metaphor, the big brick palace on the highway at Kogarah was literally the fortress from which the Saints sallied forth each week to meet and slay their opponents.

The historian Ken Inglis has argued that in Australia the Anzac tradition has acted not just as a set of nationalistic myths but as something even more culturally powerful: a 'civil religion'.[76] Increasingly, throughout the nineteenth century, the two great founding faiths of European Australia, English Protestantism and Irish Catholicism, began to dissipate in the sparse, seemingly indifferent expanse of the Australian continent. In the twentieth century, this spiritual void was filled to an extent by materialism, as the consumer products of technological modernity began to find their way into hearts and homes across the nation. Yet this still left a space for belief, and it was this space that was occupied, Inglis argues, by the iconographic, sacrificial figure of the digger, he who grew not old, but gave his life so that the nation as a whole could continue to live and to prosper.

Anyone who has ever been to an Anzac Day Dawn Service could tell you that Ken Inglis is probably right. But, while Anzac may be Australia's only fully formed example of a secular religion, in terms of the micropolitics of culture a range of other practices and activities have also worked to keep anomie at bay within what Manning Clark liked to call 'the kingdom of nothingness'.[77] Inglis is wary of conferring spiritual status on activities like football, arguing that this would be akin to declaring two-up a religious rite because the participants shout 'Jesus Christ' after the coins are tossed.[78] At the same time though, in postwar Australia, particularly in the densely populated centres of Sydney and Melbourne, football did serve as a secondary belief system of a kind. For a significant, and a very particular, fragment of the population, Australian Rules and Rugby League gave a meaning and a rhythm to life in the winter months, whereby worship took place not indoors on Sunday morning, but outside on Saturday afternoon, and the congregation waited not on the guidance of words from above, but on 'that moment of suspense about which way the ball would bounce'.[79]

There was at this time a spiritual dimension to rugby league football which, under the subsequent impact of corporate mass marketing, globalised media, television scheduling and hyper-professionalism, has largely melted away. Ironically, this climate of spirituality was at its peak in the early 1960s, even as those who ran the football codes greedily reached out towards the glittering prizes that would ultimately mean the desecration of the very thing they loved. This is why Bill Buckley called St George Leagues Club the Taj Mahal, because symbolically, even if it was ultimately just a big brick box filled with beer and poker machines, it seemed to stand for so much more.

The real Taj Mahal was built in the seventeenth century as a sarcophagus for a queen, and it is this purpose, both funereal and ethereal, as much as the overall stylistic grandeur which gives the famous structure in Agra its symbolic power. So, while comparing the two structures actually made for a ludicrous assertion, as the Taj Mahal and a Sydney leagues club weren't alike in any way at all, this is precisely why the comparison carried so much semiotic power. For those who believed in it, there was a grandeur and richness to rugby league and the life and culture associated with it; it was so much 'more than a game', and so its material symbols also found their points of resemblance, not with the ordinary and the everyday, but with the great and the worthy.

The brashness of the comparison is astounding, the self-made man casually comparing himself and his works to one of the world's great cultural and architectural treasures. And not just brash, but imperious too: competing qualities of arrogance that also, it must be admitted, often go together. But the self-made man could well afford himself such hubris in the contained, ordered world over which he presumed to rule. Inside the walls of White Australia he was building a nation anew as part of the modern world, and if it was new and modern then it must be comparable at least to the grand products of the old, foreign world, like India's most famous tourist attraction.

Personal experience played a role here too, as by this stage many men of this generation had seen some of the Old World for themselves, on military service in the Middle East and Asia, where they'd found little to weaken their belief that Australia was the best country in the world, even if it had no monuments to culture in the classical sense. And anyway, what use were monuments? This is what the generation of the self-made men's fathers, the diggers of 1915, had reasoned when they arrived in Egypt. The Pyramids hardly impressed at all; instead what most concerned them in their letters home was how 'filthy' and 'squalid' the streets were.

It is possible, of course, to see it all as just an exercise in irony, this nicknaming of the St George club the Taj Mahal. And in a sense it was ironic. But ultimately irony only works because of power relations, which is why colonised peoples are usually the most proficient practitioners of the tool. In the end, the self-made man knew he didn't possess the cultural riches of the Old World. He knew he was out on his own, and he knew that if he wanted palaces, then he was going to have to build them himself.

*

If rugby league was a form of secular religion in postwar Sydney, then St George's Taj Mahal was certainly one of its most important places of worship. Up the front steps, past the doorman with a flash of the membership badge, through the expansive foyer featuring 'Wombeyan marble floors and a deep blue textured ceiling with especially designed brass light fittings', up the internal staircase leading to the second floor, and the patron came face to face with a monumental portrait of Norm 'Sticks' Provan, the greatest Saint of all.[80] In the era of the self-made man Provan embodied St George like no one else. He was the greatest in a host of greats. Ken Kearney was too violent, Reg Gasnier too graceful, Johnny Raper too reckless, Poppa Clay too unfashionable, but the rock-like Provan – tall, powerful, fast and level-headed – was perfectly qualified to adopt the mantle. He played in the premiership-winning team of 1956 and was still there ten years later, having played in ten consecutive Grand Final wins, filling the roles of both captain and coach for the final four.

In Reg Campbell's portrait, Provan's visage impresses the viewer with its toughness. His wavy short-back-and-sides haircut, his rock jaw, strong nose, laconic mouth and firm, slightly weary gaze coalesce into an archetype of the mythic Australian male of the time, a strikingly similar face to that seen in William Dargie's 1942 Archibald Prize-winning portrait of Corporal Jim Gordon, VC (Campbell's portrait of Provan was an unsuccessful entrant in the 1965 Archibald Prize).[81] Twenty years after the end of the Second World War, Provan wears exactly the same expression as the gallant digger, his gaze both meeting the viewer's eye and yet simultaneously looking past it to some distant field of contest and victory. Indeed, the painting evokes an impressive aura. Provan is seated wearing the St George uniform, the striking red V on the plain white background, which at this time signified nothing so much as the confidence and strength generated by being on a winning streak.

According to Ian Heads in his history of the St George club, *March of the Dragons*: 'Provan was born to lead. His honesty, ambition, will to win, courage, dignity, modesty, pride in achievement, loyalty and fair play fitted him exactly for the task.'[82] As befitting his status and role in the events documented, Norm Provan provided the foreword for Heads' book. At one point he mentions the attitude of his vice-captain in the early 1960s, Billy Wilson, who, it will be remembered, would go on to lead the Bears. In the days before replacements for injured players were permissible, Wilson was famous for breaking an arm in a match and then insisting that the club doctor bind it to his body so that he could play the second half, after which he reportedly apologised to his teammates for not 'trying as hard as them'. Provan relates an anecdote concerning Wilson from a Grand Final against Western Suburbs:

> I was cut and badly concussed in the first half. At half time I was still a couple of bricks short of a pallet and Billy Wilson gave the half time address. 'We know who got Sticks . . . forget it . . . we're going out to play football,' he told us. Minutes later, Billy rendered Wests' Jim Cody horizontal and he was on his way back to the dressing room.[83]

Provan uses this anecdote to identify the qualities he feels his team-mates and club exemplified at this time: toughness, dedication and fair-mindedness, particularly in terms of a willingness to break the rules of the game in order to see justice done. Wilson performs an act of individual vengeance after urging the rest of the team to avoid such action themselves, working to achieve retribution whilst saving anyone else from the punishment of being sent from the field.

Provan's tone indicates that, on balance, such willful misbehaviour was justified, as St George's honour had been kept intact, and while they may have had to play the rest of the Grand Final a man short, they still won. Paradoxically, then, Wilson had maintained the integrity of the team through his capricious personal actions – exactly the sort of anti-authoritarian yet cause-dedicated behaviour that had traditionally been the stuff of celebratory white Australian masculinist narratives, from the work of Henry Lawson onwards. Such conduct also recalls the famous words of Captain 'Diver' Derrick, who, when ordered to withdraw from a precarious position in New Guinea in 1943, replied 'Bugger the CO', and instead led his platoon into an attack that won him a Victoria Cross.

Leaving aside the paradoxes of male honour, a remarkable metaphor can be found at play here. Provan describes himself as 'a couple of bricks short of a pallet'. Such a turn of phrase is common in idiomatic Australian: defining the subject as short of the requisite number of certain objects constituting a whole, and therefore deficient or defective in some way. Yet while the compositional possibilities of the formulation are almost limitless, it is bricks, and pallet loads of bricks, that Provan chooses to employ in the creation of this statement. Neither a couple of snags short of a barbie nor a few books short of a library, Provan writes himself as bricks short of a pallet. Bricks: the perfect metaphor for the self-made man in postwar Australia. Hard. Tough. Durable. The essence of the brick-veneer nation: each brick individual and self-contained and yet each only ever achieving any form of meaningful existence through its commingling with its fellows. Furthermore, Provan defines himself as bricks short of a pallet rather than bricks short of a wall or a house. Such fresh, virgin bricks are then pure potentiality, the perpetual clubhouse, suburb, city and nation, in a constant state of possibility, of planning, construction, and erection.

The new Club premises had actually opened for business three weeks before the official ceremony. The afternoon newspaper the *Daily Mirror* ran a five-page advertorial-style supplement containing accounts of the building's construction and features, as well as congratulatory statements in the form of advertisements from various companies involved in the creation of the club. The bricks, for example, had been sourced from a single supplier, the Punchbowl Brick and Pipe Company, and they ran the following proclamation: 'Punchbowl Brick and Pipe Co. Pty. Ltd. would like to take this opportunity to congratulate Mr. Justice and the committee of the St George Leagues Club on the completion of their new premises . . . Punchbowl Brick were proud to supply all bricks.'[84]

Punchbowl, the place where Nino Culotta performed his first day of work as a builder's labourer, didn't even lie within the boundaries of the St George district, but within the territory of neighbouring rivals Canterbury-Bankstown, the club which would eventually bring the Saints' eleven year winning streak to an end one momentous Saturday afternoon in August 1967. Nonetheless, Punchbowl Brick and Pipe's epistle sat alongside others from a range of enterprises, from that of the transnational Honeywell which supplied the office management systems to local concreters L. & A. Fazzini, suppliers of 'mechanical spray on ceilings and walls in natural or selected colours', and A. W. Hall Butchers, of Kogarah, purveyors of the meat served in the club's restaurant and bistro. In a similar style to that of the brick suppliers, most of these contractor advertisements singled out the club directors for praise along with the actual club premises.

The *Daily Mirror*'s complementary stories took a similar line, depicting the creation of the club (like 'a luxury liner') as an archetype of Australian business acumen. 'Planning for the new St George Leagues Club started in 1952', said the *Mirror*, detailing a meeting at Kogarah Oval at which 'a scheme was launched with the backing of the St George District Rugby League Football Club to establish a social club.' As so often seems to be the case in the story of private enterprise in Australia, this was painted as a humble beginning. As the newspaper put it: 'At that meeting the men had little conception that they would see such an outstanding club as the one they are to occupy from today.'[85] Again and again this had been the celebrated narrative of Anglo-Celtic Australia. From humble origins the common man had gone about his business and, depending on the circumstances, he'd battled and failed or he'd battled and won, both being noble outcomes. Ideally, he didn't do battle alone but with his mates, whether it be under the flag of the Southern Cross at Eureka, or the Union Jack at Gallipoli. And it was within this tradition that the *Daily Mirror* placed the building of the Taj Mahal, postwar temple of the average Australian. According to the newspaper, the 'Club's secret is teamwork':

> The men who made the St George Leagues Club are like the average Sydney businessman who lives next door, but with this difference – they're a dedicated team. Few are employed full-time on club business, they work during the day and give their leisure hours to the club. They look after their members, watch the pennies – as their balance sheet proves – and at the same time watch the interests of the community. No worthwhile appeal or deserving cause in the St George district has been neglected.[86]

While they may have appeared as dedicated philanthropists, in the circles in which they operated these men were anything but anonymous. On the contrary, they were a team of distinct individuals. 'Snowy' Justice, manager of the club, was 'from rugby league's school of hard knocks', had captained the St George team in the early 1930s, and then gone on to both control his own club and serve as vice-president of the New South Wales Rugby League.[87] Ernie 'Tiger' Black, who had also played with St George in the 1930s, was a prominent sports broadcaster on radio station 2KY. Frank 'Fearless' Facer, 'hard and tough and ruthless', had a famous stint playing with the club in the late 1940s, after being poached from the luckless Bears.[88] Others, like Alex Mackie, Glyn Price and Laurie Doust, had previously played key roles in club management. Yet despite the strength of their individual profiles, the crucial point was their mutual commitment. As Frank Facer put it, what distinguished St George and accounted for their success was 'absolute dedication to the club, total involvement'.[89] Now, in July 1963, this allegiance had paid off. As the *Mirror* saw it, 'Today at 10 a.m. the ideas of the seventeen men who met in the training room of the Jubilee Oval early in 1952 have come to fruition in a building described by the fans as a sportsman's club that cannot be equalled.'[90]

*

In *A Thousand Plateaus*, Deleuze and Guattari famously oppose the concepts 'tree' and 'rhizome'. Trees, they argue, are unitary, singular, fixed, forever reproducing their hierarchical systems. Rhizomes, by contrast, are disordered, variegated and expansive, and connect any point with any other given point: they have no beginning and no end. To think and act rhizomatically, Deleuze and Guattari argue, to follow lines of flight, provides a way of resisting both the order of the micropolitics of the social field, and the apparatus of the state.[91]

Maybe, maybe not, but if we take a step backwards from this celebrated opposition of the taproot and the rhizome, yet stay within the theoretical world of binary opposites, we can also productively oppose the images of the tree and the brick. In an Australia suffused by the glow of the postwar suburban dream, it was in fact the tree that was the signifier of disorder and chaos. Trees seemed to cover so much of the nation's potentially productive space in a tangled and cluttered weave. Bricks conversely – solid, durable, inflexible – seemed nothing less than the material source of progress, both individually and nationally. Spreading out from the centre of the city, sturdy brick constructions dominated land recently cleared of useless, unproductive scrub and bush. Fittingly, after retiring from football Norm Provan became a prominent and successful retailer of white goods, a purveyor of the everyday functional objects that filled the brick suburban homes. However, it's notable that when called upon to do so, it is the metaphor of the brick rather than that of the refrigerator or washing machine, which he employed to describe himself as a footballer in the early 1960s.

79

Bricks, rugby league, entrepreneurial business activity, they all fitted together neatly and profitably in this particular place at this particular moment in Australian cultural history. The bricks made by the Punchbowl Brick and Pipe Company gave material form to the success story that was the St George Leagues Club, which was in turn built on the sporting success of the rugby league team, with both club and team overseen by the same group of enterprising men. Like bricks, these men didn't stand alone, but rather worked together. As the *Daily Mirror* put it, the secret of their success lay with the fact that they were 'a dedicated team'. In this sense, and irrespective of their actual political leanings, they were the antithesis of the sort of shadowy gang exemplified by Labor's faceless men. The St George men by contrast were individuals, each one successful in his own right, just like the 'average Sydney businessman next door', yet at the same time they were all committed to their mutual cause, and to each other.

As the *Mirror*'s account illustrated, these men were pillars of the community, and while they weren't afraid to show their faces, they were also humble enough to keep things in perspective. Such qualities, emblematic of the self-made man, were also perfectly demonstrated by Keith Milburn, a Sydney-based concreter, whose company was awarded the tender for the construction of the US Navy's North West Cape base on the same day the St George Leagues Club was officially opened. Under the headline 'The Drake Touch', the *Sun-Herald* gave the following account:

> A few hours after hearing yesterday that he had won the £15 and a half million contract to build the first stage of the Americans' radio base in Western Australia, placid Keith Milburn, 55, went for his normal Saturday bowls. Mr Milburn is head of the Sydney firms Concrete Industries (Monier) Ltd., and its subsidiary Hutchison Bros. 'I'm

delighted, of course,' Mr Milburn said, 'but I'm not missing my bowls
because of it.'[92]

The *Sunday Telegraph* ran a similar story, accompanied by a photograph of Keith Milburn in action, 'rolling one down at Epping bowling club'.[93] The image drew on a famous Anglo-Saxon antecedent,
as referenced by the *Sun-Herald*: the unruffled Sir Francis Drake
announcing in 1588 that he would finish his game of bowls before
dealing with the invading Spaniards. Keith Milburn's responsibilities
involved an entirely different armada, the US Navy's intercontinental
ballistic missile submarine fleet, and his task wasn't to conquer it but
rather to facilitate its operations. Nonetheless Milburn was as equally
circumspect in relation to his duty as the great Elizabethan military
adventurer had been and, despite the fact that he was now in charge
of Australia's biggest construction job and in partnership with the
world's biggest and most powerful navy, there was no way he was
going to forgo his Saturday afternoon game with the boys in order to
fret over the details.

This image of Keith Milburn on the bowling green perfectly
captures the Australian experience of the Menzies years: continu-
ing to cling to the cultural traditions of Britain while the political
realities of the Cold War pushed the country into an ever-increasing
military entanglement with the United States. Robert Menzies literally embodied such circumstances, regularly receiving royal hon-
ours from the British while forging alliances with the Americans. For
archetypal common man Keith Milburn though, it was simply a case
of enjoying his usual weekend recreation before getting on with the
job he knew best: concreting. That ever-so-English of activities, lawn
bowls, was one of the most beloved pastimes of the older Australian
male, blessed as he was with the climate, leisure time, and leveling
social democratic ethos that allowed the sport to flourish. Naturally
enough, then, the St George Leagues Club complex included two

bowling greens. So while the bowlers may have all had Australian accents, and sweated it out under the relentless Australian sun, and despite the experiences of Gallipoli and Pozieres and Tobruk and Kokoda, and all our attempts to forge some form of national identity of our own, in a way every bowl sent down the green still carried with it the echo of Sir Francis Drake.[94]

Similarly, for the laconic Keith Milburn North West Cape was just another concreting job, no more, no less. Just another exercise in development and construction at yet another remote location, as far removed both physically and psychologically from the national centres of population as that patch of Cape York jungle destroyed by the bomb test. Yet in some ways this particular concreting job would impact upon the nation like no other, inextricably tying Australia into America's global military network, making it both a front-line nuclear target for the USSR and a front-line communications centre for any military action initiated by the United States.

These were the issues that had plunged the Labor Party into such ideological turmoil, the issues that Alan Reid had exploited in the *Daily Telegraph*, the issues that had put Calwell and Whitlam on the street corner outside the Hotel Kingston while the faceless men thrashed things out inside. These were the same issues that had enabled Menzies to regain his control of Australia's political agenda during 1963, and lock the nation into a defensive union with the Americans that would result in young, conscripted Australian soldiers being sent to fight in Vietnam some two years later. And soon, more such concreting jobs would follow, at Nurrangar, and at Pine Gap.

For the self-made man such complexities of domestic and international politics would ultimately be resolved in the most practical fashion: by cutting down more trees, pouring more concrete, laying more bricks, and then settling back to enjoy a couple of beers, or a bit of a game, be it football, cricket, bowls or whatever. As Monty Porter, a plumber, and another St George player of the golden era put it:

> The St George football team dominated my life for nine years. I really enjoyed the routine although it might sound a bit boring: Saturday — the game, mostly at the SCG; booze it up on Saturday night. A barbecue about every third Sunday. Monday — to work or to the NSWRL doctor . . . Tuesday night — to training and a few beers (no breathalyser!). Thursday night — training and a couple of drinks over which the forthcoming game was discussed. Friday — early night.[95]

The self-made man was simply getting on with his life within the cultural parameters of his time, but his activities weren't neutral, and they were giving the nation a very precise and particular form. While scientists and military men blew away the uncivilised chaos of the bush, and Robert Menzies harried the faceless men of the Labor Party, a dedicated group of Sydney businessmen built St George's Taj Mahal, and a concrete company got ready to build an American communications base. Meanwhile, men like Norm Provan understood themselves as bricks in a much greater structure, one that ultimately gave their lives both a measure and a meaning.

1. Arthur and his friend Phyllis at the Fowler Potteries Annual Ball, 1939

2. Frederick McCubbin's The Pioneer (1904).
National Gallery of Victoria

3. Patrick White milks his cow 'The Dream of Penrith' at Castle Hill in the 1950s. National Library of Australia

4. Walter Chiari and John Meillon knock 'em back in Michael Powell's film of *They're a Weird Mob*, 1965.

5. John O'Grady on the Great Barrier Reef in 1965. National Archives of Australia

6. 'Just like the average businessman next door':
the St. George rugby league team after the 1959 Grand Final.

7. Kogarah's 'Taj Mahal', photographed by Joan Hatton in 1968.
Kogarah Local Studies Centre

8. Reg Campbell's portrait of Norm Provan, a contender for the 1965 Archibald Prize.

9. 'A distinctive quality so strikingly obvious': a Coonawarra Wines advertisement from the pages of *Meanjin*, 1964.

Dedicated to exploring and developing Australia's
immense mineral and industrial reserves, C.R.A., like
Meanjin, seeks to uncover the hidden potential of this
continent, and provide the means whereby both industry
and the arts can enrich the life of our community.
CONZINC RIOTINTO OF AUSTRALIA LIMITED

explore
ROSELANDS
Australia's greatest
shopping-community
centre

10. Penetrating the text:
Conzinc Riotinto Australia
advertises in *Meanjin* in 1964.

11. 'So new, so modern … so exciting':
a Sydney newspaper advertisement
celebrating the opening of Roselands.
National Archives of Australia

12. Roselands' central court in 1965, with the Raindrop Fountain
in the left foreground. National Archives of Australia

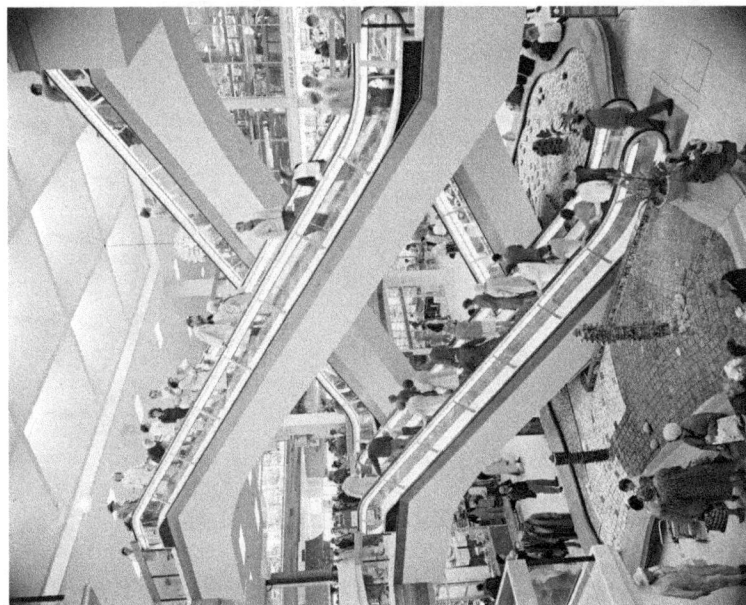

13. Roselands: 'the lure and bustle of a bazaar in a twentieth-century setting'. National Archives of Australia

14. The 'Hotel Australia', photographed by Kerry and Co, Sydney, circa 1891-1917. Museum of Applied Arts and Social Sciences

15. Prime Minister Menzies ponders the question 'What's better than beer?' at a function at the Australia Hotel 1962. State Library of New South Wales

16. The Long Bar of the Australia Hotel in the 1950s, featuring ceiling designs by Lucien Henry. Museum of Applied Arts and Social Sciences

17. Rowe Street circa 1950, featuring the salon of Parisian milliner Henriette Lamotte (also known as the Countess D'Espinay), next door to the Roycroft Library, which was known for its collection of very modern books. State Library of New South Wales

18. Harry Seidler's MLC Centre, photographed by Max Dupain in 1978.
State Library of New South Wales/Penelope Seidler

5. A Record of Barbarism

'To progress, a nation must develop culturally as well as industri-ally.'[96] You can find this statement in the March 1964 issue of the Australian literary journal *Meanjin Quarterly*. It's a simple assertion, typical of the tone and concerns that found expression in the writings of Australian academics and cultural commentators working in the middle years of the twentieth century. As Donald Horne put it in *The Lucky Country*: 'the basis of material prosperity in the future is likely to lie, for the first time in history, with clever, educated people.'[97] But despite its similarity to declarations such as Horne's, the asser-tion drawn from *Meanjin* isn't lifted from a work of social analysis. It is the opening line of an advertisement for General Motors Holden (GMH), an advertisement that details the global car company's finan-cial support for Australian theatre via its sponsorship of a prize, the 'GMH Theatre Award'.

The advertisement continues: 'General Motors Holden estab-lished, in 1958, the GMH Theatre Award to aid the development of the Australian theatre and, in particular, to encourage Australian creative talent.' The copy then lists the creators of the musicals that received the 1962 awards, and concludes by announcing the closing date for entries for 1963, and the fact that the trophy for first prize is designed by the Australian modernist sculptor Lyndon Dadswell. There is also a graphic illustrating the trophy.[98]

In terms of form and structure, the demarcation line between advertising and the scholarly essays, reviews and short fiction making up an issue of *Meanjin* at this time is obvious. The advertisements are clearly marked out by both their product names and their design, and they announce themselves clearly to their audience. Similarly the academic essays obey the established laws of content and layout, *as do* the reviews, short stories and poems, leaving the reader in no doubt as to which genre they belong to. The lines never blur, and nor should they be expected to. This was 1964, and *Meanjin* was no radical piece of experimentation, but a serious journal of arts and letters. Anyway, the days of casually fusing article and advert, and of the submission of information to layout, were still a decade or two away in the future that was to follow modernism.

In terms of content though, the borders dividing up the textual fabric of *Meanjin* aren't nearly so clear-cut. On the facing page to the GMH Theatre Award advertisement, *Meanjin*'s helmsman Clem Christensen gives both an outline and a critique of the recently published *Tauber Report* into the state of Australian libraries. He writes:

> The Tauber Report is, in fact, only one of a long series of reports dating from 1955, which have all deplored the poverty of Australia's libraries in the most critical terms. That such reports should continue almost unchanged in purport after Australia has experienced a long period of unprecedented prosperity surely points to the disgraceful fact that library development in Australia is still inhibited by apathy and neglect, when it should be leaping to keep pace with the nation's phenomenal development in almost every other sphere.[99]

Prosperity, leaping to keep pace, the nation's phenomenal development: these are, as we know, key elements of the cultural shorthand of the period. These are also the ideas and values that motivated the self-made man to clear trees and pour concrete, though in this case they empower and animate Christensen's opinions on library stock – so much so that it, too, appears as a commodity of vital national importance, just like coalmines and steelworks and car factories. If their Theatre Award is anything to go by these sentiments would, no doubt, have been shared by the board of directors of GMH.

Compare it to any other copy of *Meanjin* from the early 1960s and you'll see that the March 1964 edition is a fairly typical example of the form this journal took at the time. Now while, as previously mentioned, in formal terms the individual texts contained in the journal appear very distinct, mainly due to their generic differences (essay, review, short story, poem, advertisement), within the realm of what we might call the embodiment of ideas they share a lot of common ground. For, despite their differences, there is a level on which the differing texts are all speaking the same language: articulating a roughly consensual conception of the idea of Australia, the social position of individuals within the nation, the nation's place in the world, and its direction in relation to the governing notions of progress. As a result, I'd suggest that an examination of some of these advertisements and articles, and the context in which they exist – the journal, its readership, the academic system – can show us the manner in which the ideals of progress, individual identity and nation building that are embodied in both *The Tree of Man* and *They're a Weird Mob* also animate this review of arts and letters.

This is a theoretical position that generally accepts that texts embody ideas, rather than the other way around. Raymond Williams, the key figure in the development of cultural studies in Britain, put it this way:

> . . . in any society, in any particular period, there is a central system of practices, meanings and values, which we can properly call dominant and effective. This implies no presumption about its value. All I am saying is that it is central . . . the central, effective and dominant system

of meanings and values, which are not merely abstract but which are organised and lived.[100]

Williams wrote these words in the 1970s, in an essay called 'Base and Superstructure in Marxist Cultural Theory'. In it he pays a lot of attention to what he calls the 'process of interpretation': the means, in other words, by which the 'dominant system of culture' speaks itself, and the mechanisms by which 'it' addresses its 'audience'. Across the broad range of education and knowledge systems within a society, Williams argues, and at various points within the group of institutions we term the media, this dominant system of culture can be found at work constantly creating, recreating and circulating the set of meanings and values necessary to everyday political and economic life.[101] While both the visibility of these mechanisms and the level of intensity of their articulation of the 'dominant' may vary from one site of announcement to another, their role in the maintenance of the status quo remains constant.

Generally, I find myself in agreement with Williams, though rather than employ the term 'dominant', with all its totalising implications, I'd prefer to use 'ideal', or 'ideal type'. It is the *ideal* of nation building and progress that finds expression in these texts in question, and it is an *ideal type* of culture, of economic, political and social values, which underpins them. I'd also want to move away from the idea of culture being understood as anything as well organised as a 'system', as for me it seems much more like a loose grouping of often cooperative though sometimes competitive forces and interests. Nonetheless, I'd argue that the basic premise outlined by Williams, of analysing society and culture via an examination of the articulation of a central set of practices and values, remains a great analytic tool. Indeed, it is a tool I intend to continue to apply to this issue of *Meanjin*.

The March 1964 *Meanjin* commences with an essay by Martin Boyd, in which he defines his role as a novelist as dealing with 'the interplay of human souls and bodies'.[102] In another essay, Bernard Smith speculates on the fate of the funds donated to Sydney University as part of the Power Bequest. In other articles Anne Bavinton analyses Christopher Brennan's 'Lilith' poems, Derek Stanford contributes a piece on the poet David Gascoigne, and Keith Macartney scrutinises a production of the Patrick White play, *A Cheery Soul*. Lastly, the book review section deals with *Cooper's Creek* by Alan Moorehead, and *Paintings of Tom Roberts* by Robert Campbell. Finally, Peter Cowan and John Bellair contribute short stories written in what we could call, after Henry Lawson, the classic Australian realist style, while Tom Shapcott and Gwen Harwood publish poetry in the issue.

In terms of an exercise in historically informed textual analysis, the items listed above are of great interest individually. However, as I want to interpret the March 1964 *Meanjin* as a textually divergent but at the same time conceptually coherent whole, I'm just as interested in the advertisements and the ideas and values they embody as in the articles and stories. In addition to the announcement of the GMH Theatre Award, the March 1964 *Meanjin* contains a number of other advertisements for services and products. Some, such as an ad for the *Australian Journal of French Studies*, or for new books by publishers Rigby and Angus & Robertson, appeal directly to what we could call *Meanjin*'s standard readership of professional intellectuals. *Indonesia* for example, a geographical and political study by Bruce Grant, is promoted this way: 'Our nearest neighbour, with its 100 million people on 3,000 islands, is of direct concern to every thinking Australian.'[103] Other advertisements, such as those for the International Harvester Company, and for the mining multinational Conzinc Riotinto, instead employ more hard-working copy tailored specifically for a journal of cultural issues, as they need to bridge a bigger gap between product and reader: between the fields of mining and primary production, on the one hand, and literature and the arts, on the other.

Falling between these two different styles is an advertisement for Coonawarra Estate Claret. It occupies the first page of the journal, and is composed of two illustrations and a blurb assembled from a mix of historical and technical information. Simultaneously situated within the pages of *Meanjin* and within the broader cultural context of the period, this advertisement tells us quite a bit about certain aspects of class and capital in Australia at the time. The title of the ad is 'The Coonawarra Estate':

> COONAWARRA is on the extreme southern edge of the viticultural zone where grapes ripen very slowly due to the cool climate. The grapes are small, thick-skinned and flavour-rich with the low sugar and high acid that distinguish the great table wines of the world. To make the most of the unique qualities with which Coonawarra grapes have been endowed we have restored the age-old laborious task of paddling.
>
> Paddling consists of plunging down the marc with long-handled wooden paddles to keep it continually submerged in the fermenting must, thus fully extracting the latent qualities in the Coonawarra Estate Hermitage and Cabernet Sauvignon grapes.
>
> The distinctive quality of Coonawarra Estate Claret is in part due to this painstaking practice, one of several hand-methods employed. One need not be a connoisseur to find the subtle flavour and bouquet in Coonawarra Estate Claret – it is all so strikingly obvious, a great joy to all those who appreciate a good red wine.[104]

Accompanied by a drawing of four rustic-looking men performing the task of paddling, together with an illustration of a 1956 bottle of Coonawarra Claret, the advertisement targets both the experienced and informed wine consumer ('a great joy to those who appreciate a good red wine') and the novice ('one need not be a connoisseur to find the subtle flavour'). If this is the case, then the ad is well placed within *Meanjin*, a journal that, while an archetypal exercise in intellectualism, was always moderately left, and never snobbish, elitist or conservative.

We can call the modes of textual construction organising *Meanjin* and directly articulated in the Coonawarra advertisement both progressive *and* democratic: there is the inclusion of enough technical detail and description of the production process to satisfy the initiated while still inviting the uninitiated – an approach designed to appeal to as broad a cross-section of the community as possible. At the same time, this is precisely the type of reading we produce when we pull a text out of its context of publication and circulation. For, even though we may analyse the text in question in terms of the social constructions of knowledge that it embodies (notions of history, of value, and so on), we also need to examine it in terms of publication and circulation, as no text ever exists in a vacuum. In other words, what we also need to address, along with the meanings we perceive within it, are questions such as: Who has access to it? Who will actually get to read it? And how will it speak to them?

The key here is the position of wine as a beverage within Australian society in the 1950s and early 1960s. Wine, like all objects of consumption, was, and still is, both a commodity and a signifier of value. Throughout the nineteenth century wine was consistently produced in what are still the principal Australian vineyard districts in New South Wales, Victoria and South Australia. At this time, though, the wine made was destined mainly for export to England, with domestic wine consumption being quite limited and generally restricted to fortified varieties with a very high alcohol content. The most popular beverage consumed in Australia up until the Second World War was, of course, beer, but a shortage of beer during the war years sent the consumption of wine up dramatically, with Australians going from drinking 14.5 million litres of wine in 1939 to 37 million litres in 1944. However, after the war, as wine industry historian Phillip

Murphy notes, 'most Australians went back to drinking beer and looked on wine as something either remote if it was table wine, or slightly sinister if it was port or sherry.'[106]

Which brings us back to the self-made man. In 1964 the consumption and appreciation of table wine in Australia was almost exclusively the prerogative of the middle and upper classes, existing in direct opposition to the consumption of that most ubiquitous working-class beverage, beer. Indeed, the two drinks were almost binary opposites, particularly from a working-class point of view. For the self-made man the refined practice of wine drinking was, at best, an irrelevant predilection of the toffs, and at worst yet another questionable activity engaged in by the ever-growing population of 'New Australians'. On the whole, it appeared as both un-manly and un-Australian, and we can find a clear illustration of this attitude in *Cop This Lot*, John O'Grady's 1960 sequel to *They're a Weird Mob*:

> 'Wot's better than beer?' Pat asked.
>
> 'Vino. Vin rouge. Rotwein. The civilised and incomparable juice of the grape.'
>
> 'Gees,' Pat said. 'Yer don't mean bloody plonk, do yer?' 'Vino bianco col amaro,' Joe said.
>
> 'Same ter you, whatever 'ut means. Never thought I'd see the day. Me old mates slingin' orf at beer. Man shoulda stayed in the bush.'[107]

Cop This Lot was also a great popular success, even though it failed to match the extraordinary sales figures of the first Culotta novel. This is understandable, as most of the book's action is set not in Australia but in Italy, a premise which would no doubt have curtailed its appeal, given the attitude of many Anglo-Celts to the land of the New Australian. Indeed, as Nino's mate and former boss Joe says of Italy: 'Must be somethin' wrong with 'ut orright, or your mob wouldn't all be leavin' 'ut and comin' 'ere.'[108] Despite such misgivings, though, Joe agrees to accompany Nino on a visit to Milano to see his ailing father. Another of their building industry mates, Dennis, is also recruited for the trip, despite Nino's fear that 'I do not think he will like Italy'. So off they go, on a Qantas Super Constellation to Fiji and then a cargo ship for the rest of the trip, having forgone the much simpler option of a direct passenger liner from Sydney because on board such a ship 'you had to dress for dinner'.

As is to be expected, Joe and Dennis spend much of their time in Italy cynically observing the natives in the laconic Australian fashion, hence the book's title. A major preoccupation is their ultimately futile search for 'decent tucker' such as steak and eggs and something to drink other than 'plonk'. As Nino observes in Milano:

> The subject of beer was uppermost in Joe's mind. He would not accept my statement that draught beer was unavailable . . .
>
> So while the rest of us were shopping, and visiting the Automobile Club, Joe spent most of the day wandering from one bar to another looking for beer. He did not find any.[109]

Pat, their other building industry mate, had declined to accompany them on the trip to Italy, and it is at a barbecue back in Bankstown held to celebrate the return of the travellers that he asks the question quoted earlier: 'What's better than beer?' In this, the concluding scene of the book, Dennis and Joe appear to have adopted European manners, taste and lifestyle in the course of their journey. While the rest of the boys stand around the keg in the garage the two returned travellers refuse the schooners offered to them and instead spend most of their time inside the house dressed in their new Italian suits, sipping wine and being polite to the women. But this ends up being exposed as an elaborate practical joke, and the narrative is finally resolved by the pair of pseudo-European sophisticates admitting that they are only kidding, swapping their suits for shorts and singlets, and then getting stuck into the grog out the back.

Like its predecessor *They're a Weird Mob*, even a cursory examination of *Cop This Lot* raises a range of questions for the cultural historian in relation to issues of patriarchy, ethnocentrism, national and cultural identity, the class system, the ownership of capital, and the building of Australian suburbia in the 1950s and 1960s. Yet while all of these factors are interrelated, it is the class system and its relationship to the circulation of objects and commodities within Australian society at the time that I'm most interested in here. If we contrast *Cop This Lot* with the March 1964 issue of *Meanjin* we can see that in the same place (southeastern Australia), at the same time (the early 1960s), the same commodity and the practices of consumption associated with it appear in two different texts in mutually exclusive terms. In looking at this situation from the perspective of the critical position outlined earlier – taking into account the ideal 'system of practices, meanings and values' in circulation at the time – the obvious conclusion is not the fact that the texts are simply saying different things, but that they are saying different things because, as texts, they are used for entirely different purposes by their readers and consumers.

I'm not the only person whose attention has been caught by the placing of this advertisement for Wynn's Coonawarra Claret in *Meanjin*. Writing a history of the Coonawarra viticultural region in 1989, the wine critic James Halliday mentions the very same advertisement as he outlines Wynn's marketing strategy in the 1950s and 1960s: 'Next, Wynn embarked on an advertising campaign in such unlikely magazines as *Quadrant* and *Meanjin*, which quite by chance formed part of my university life when I studied arts in 1956'.[110]

For me, this is a remarkable observation. Halliday sees *Quadrant* as an 'unlikely' venue for such an advertisement. What then would he consider to have been a 'likely' location for an ad for Coonawarra Claret at this time, *Rugby League Week?* Similarly remarkable is his relaxed, casual observation that *Quadrant* and *Meanjin* were 'quite by chance' a part of his life as an arts student in the 1950s. Contrary to this being a 'chance' relationship, I'd suggest that any Australian arts student of the late 1950s (particularly one headed for a career in the establishment) who wasn't paying attention to *Meanjin* and, in particular, to the conservative mouthpiece *Quadrant* certainly wouldn't be getting a Distinction for their work in 'Great Novels Embodying Universal Human Values', or whatever it was their English department course was called.

James Halliday's happy-go-lucky recollections of the coincidences of life as a young bourgeois are immediately undermined in the next sentence by his own definition of the Wynn company marketing strategy: 'it was always intended that the wines from the Coonawarra Estate would be positioned at the very top end of the market'.[111] Contrary to Halliday's belief in chance encounters, there was nothing in the manner of chance or coincidence in his simultaneous youthful encounter with *Meanjin* and Wynn's Claret. As he says, the wines were intended for the 'top end of the market', and this was a place where, it almost goes without saying, one also led the literary life at university back in the days when such institutions were few in number in Australia, and the vast majority of those in attendance came from comfortable families able to afford the fees, not to mention the expensive private school which generally served as preparation for varsity life. Antithetical to chance relationships, then, this was a time when wine and literary journals went hand in hand, just like bricklaying and beer.

If we look from an analytic rather than emotive perspective at the choice a drinker made between beer and wine in Australia in the early 1960s, we can see this choice as one facet of Williams' 'organised and lived' collection of 'meanings and values'. If we want to go further down the analytic track, we can also draw on the French sociologist Pierre Bourdieu's argument that what such a choice represents is the 'relationship that is actually established between the pertinent characteristics of economic and social condition . . . and the distinctive features associated with the corresponding position in the universe of life-styles'.[112]

In his landmark work, *Distinction: A Social Critique of the Judgement of Taste*, Bourdieu draws on a mass of sociological fieldwork done on patterns of consumption in 1960s France to argue that questions like the one posed above – the choice for an Australian of the period of wine or beer – represent not just the unmotivated personal exercise of an inclination towards a particular beverage, but an organised selection motivated by, among other factors, a person's income, occupation, class position, gender, social and familial history, and level of education. For Bourdieu, the classification and selection of objects for consumption 'is the product of the internalization of the structure of social space, in the form in which it impinges through the experience of a particular position in that space'.

In other words, in class-based consumer society, our wants and choices are never totally 'free' as such, but grow out of our social status and social actions. Accordingly, social life 'continuously transforms necessities into strategies, constraints into preferences, and, without any mechanical determination, it generates the set of "choices" constituting life-styles, which derive their meaning, i.e., their value, from their position in a system of oppositions and correlations'.[113] Despite the apparent rigidity of this description, the social and cultural net that generates and orders our choices is actually quite flexible, even as it is simultaneously constraining. As Bourdieu says, rather than simply being an inflexible mechanical construction, some sort of imprisoning form of superstructure rigidly erected on an economic base, social life presents us instead with a continuous range of motivated choices. Subsequently, the way we exercise our choices within this classificatory network is often referred to as *taste*. At the same time though, as Bourdieu sees it, the 'universe' of taste works as both an organiser for, and as an organisation of, meaning within a society and culture.

There is, necessarily, an economic relationship at work here, as there is in all aspects of life in consumer capitalist society, because a desire for and appreciation of a particular object, product or practice always exists in relation to its availability. In other words, the more easily available and therefore less expensive something is, then the more likely it is to fit into a pattern of working-class tastes, while the more expensive, the more difficult to obtain an object or practice is, then the more likely it is to form a meaningful part of an affluent middle-class lifestyle. While such paraphrasing inevitably simplifies both the issues involved and Bourdieu's complex and nuanced mode of analysis, we can still confidently assert that, in general, taste and lifestyle are never simply pastimes, but social regulators as well. For Bourdieu, taste provides

> a sort of social orientation, a 'sense of one's place', guiding the occupants of a given place in social space towards the social positions adjusted to their properties, and towards the practices or goods which befit the occupants of that position. It implies a practical anticipation of what the social meaning and value of the chosen practice or thing will probably be, given their distribution in social space and the practical knowledge the other agents have of the correspondence between goods and groups . . .
>
> The cognitive structures which social agents implement in their practical knowledge of the social world are internalized, 'embodied' social structures . . . Being the product of the incorporation of the fundamental structures of a society, these principles of division are common to all agents of

the society and make possible the production of a common, meaningful world, a common-sense world.[114]

This is the essence of Bourdieu's concept of cultural capital, and the way that an individual's investment in whatever kind of cultural capital they value and desire, from literary magazines to greyhound racing formguides, is directly related to the complex nuances of their level of economic capital. It is therefore these 'internalised' social structures and the 'common-sense world' they generate that prompts Pat to ask 'What's better than beer': a rhetorical question, in fact, because in the world of John O'Grady and Nino Culotta, the world of the self-made man, there is *nothing* better than beer.

They are of course 'free' to choose to drink anything they wish, but for a whole range of historical, economic and climatic reasons to do with the availability of ingredients, the technologies of production, and a working life spent largely in a lather of sweat under a hot sun (the thirst-quenching and physical stress-numbing properties of beer in this circumstance being unmatched by most other drinks), they are bound to choose beer. This, by the way, in a geographic sense, turns Bourdieu's findings on working-class drinking habits on their head, as cheap table wine has traditionally been the staple of the workers of France, though this is an inversion that only serves to validate the analytic method: again, in France, a different set of circumstances (a cool climate, bountiful irrigation, a diet rich in saturated fats) has historically driven the widespread, populist consumption of wine rather than beer.

Similarly, in a certain sense there is nothing really free or open in Wynn's invitation to all those 'who appreciate a good red wine'. For this call to participate is as much a device for setting limits as it is the platform for an offer open to all, with the verb *appreciate* working on at least two levels here. Ostensibly, appreciation of the product may be a possibility for all consumers, but in this particular case it

105

requires knowledge of a set of codes and practices of interpretation understood by the few rather than the many. In a sense, this offer to participate actually propagates an elitism that is in direct contradiction to *Meanjin*'s intended democratic, pluralist ideals. One may not necessarily have needed to be a connoisseur to appreciate the 1956 claret, but the circumstances outlined above dictated that those *in the know* would be in the best position to do so. And the implication is obvious here. In the same vein, one needn't have been a connoisseur of literature to appreciate *Meanjin*, but it certainly helped, as the 'review of arts and letters' was never intended as a mass-market publication.

As markers for defining one's sense of place within Australia in the early 1960s, a society so often referred to as classless, both the barbecue scene in *Cop This Lot* and the Wynn's Coonawarra advertisement in *Meanjin* are strikingly effective. Wine and wine drinkers may be the butt of numerous jokes in *Cop This Lot*, and yet, at the very same moment, the same social and cultural forces are also hard at work combining a good red wine and a particular style of literary criticism in a powerful alliance.

*

So, what about the particular form of literary criticism found in *Meanjin* at this time? What has it got to do with the ethic of the self-made man, and the ideologies of national progress and development?

Broadly, we can define the house style popular at *Meanjin* in the early 1960s as one very much grounded in an Australian social realist approach to writing. Social realism – a distant, less explicitly political relative of Marxist socialist realism, with an emphasis on realist narratives dealing with quotidian dilemmas – was the preferred genre of most of the generation of fiction authors who had figured prominently in *Meanjin* since the 1940s. These included Gavin Casey, Peter

Cowan and Vance Palmer, as well as David Martin (Ludwig Detsinyi), John Morrison, Judah Waten and even Katharine Susannah Prichard, who were all members of the communist Realist Writers Group.

At the same time, though, this preference for realism also sat alongside, and sometimes even mixed with, critical practices derived from so-called New Criticism, which emerged as a methodological orthodoxy in British and American English departments in the mid-twentieth century. As an approach to reading, New Criticism represented a kind of formalism that tended to detach the literary text from its social and historical contexts, turning it into a self-enclosed artifact. At some (but by no means all) points, New Criticism intersected with Leavisism, the critical style established by the influential Cambridge critic F.R. Leavis and his wife Q.D. Leavis. Where New Criticism was quasi-scientific in its attitude to literary works, Leavisism was essentially a mode of moral criticism, concerned with the identification of Great Literature: an object defined via the categories passion, grace, sensibility and spirit. What aligned the two movements was an emphasis on 'close reading': deep analysis of the text alone at the expense of its contexts. Now, while social realism and 'close reading' may seem a rather unlikely mix, in the relative cultural isolation of Australia at the time these two erstwhile opposites managed to cooperate well enough.

A good example of an activist literary criticism in the New Critical tradition from the March 1964 *Meanjin* is 'The Darkness of Brennan's "Lilith"', an analysis by Anne Bavinton of the 'Lilith' series of poems from Christopher Brennan's *Poems 1913*. Bavinton's twin aims in the article are to defend Australia's leading metaphysical poet against the charge of 'obscurity' (such behaviour being a sin for New Critics and social realists alike), while considering prosecuting him for something else: this being that, 'the poet's failure to make the subject of the poem able to be discovered by an attentive reader would mean the failure of the poem'. Bavinton goes on though to determine that Brennan 'is not guilty' of such obscurantism, as he provides clues to what the Lilith symbol actually means (the unpacking of symbols being a key New Critical strategy).

The Lilith referred to by Brennan is, Bavinton says, a figure of Hebrew myth. Indeed, she was Adam's first wife, who left the Garden of Eden after refusing the role of subservient woman. Lilith appears in the first part of Goethe's *Faust* and, prefiguring Brennan, in English she was subject to the pens of Dante Gabriel Rossetti and Robert Browning. Bavinton argues that Brennan's series of poems provide an insight into the manner in which 'both vision and the poetic imagination perceive spiritual reality'. For Bavinton the 'Lilith' poems' 'defect' isn't 'obscurity', but something else, a 'lack' of definite conclusions as to 'the basic presentation of spiritual reality'. She continues: 'while Brennan represents Unknown Spiritual Reality by means of the Lilith symbol, he does not really make any verifiable statement concerning the nature or content of this subject.' Ultimately, Christopher Brennan's 'failure' lies with the fact that his poems aren't 'resolved in any terms that penetrate to the significance *behind* the Lilith myth'.[115]

Penetration. This is a key critical concept central to both this cultural period and this genre of criticism. Great works of art, so said the argument, were ones that penetrated the fog of the prosaic to expose the transcendental truths of human nature and existence. Similarly, great critics penetrated the surface of such artworks in order to know their meaning and thereby determine their greatness or, alternately, their lack of greatness. And so it went.

Nowadays, after a few decades of poststructuralist and postmodern literary and cultural theory, it's relatively easy to sit back and sarcastically pull such critical work apart. It is inherently conservative, we say; it is self-satisfied; it declares a particular point of view to be universal; it reifies a white, male, middle-class experience of the world. Indeed, it probably is and does all of these things, but we also need to remind ourselves that it was also culturally relative, in that it made sense in its time and place, it didn't simply stand alone outside society, waiting for some smartarse cultural theorist to come along and ridicule it. And, if it is indeed possible to do that now, that's primarily because the predominant social and cultural fabric has changed so much.

But let us get back to penetration. It is of course a key unit of currency in a patriarchal libidinal economy. In the New Critical tradition, it was the role of the ruthless individualist critic, armed with the hard phallus of refined analytical logic, to penetrate the murky depths of the text. And the text, back before its liberation at the hands of French post-structuralism, had no option other than to lie there and take it. As I said, it's easy to get carried away with such sarcasm, but that doesn't alter the fact that an ability to penetrate is the crucial component Anne Bavinton sees as necessary to a successful piece of literature, and which she herself, just like any hyper-aggressive male critic, applies to Christopher Brennan's 'Lilith' poems.

It is the concept of penetration as a form of literary and intellectual action that gives Bavinton's argument its rationale. This is a crucial point because, in another part of this issue of *Meanjin*, the idea of penetration, the promise of penetrating the darkness and reaching the riches within, is also used to structure an advertisement, in this case one for Conzinc Riotinto Australia (CRA), subsidiary of the British transnational mining giant Conzinc Riotinto. Occupying a full page, the advert is symmetrical, with two large arrows with rounded points moving upwards and downwards from a written text. This is a display of dynamism and energy. The head of each arrow (penis) contains a round CRA logo (a symbol of potency set to impregnate the virgin Australian landmass). Two photographs accompany and substantiate this imagery. In the subterranean half of the graphic assemblage a man, a miner, wields a heavy instrument, an actual machine for penetrating the darkness of the unknown earth, and he goes about his penetrative task with the calm determination of the quiet achiever. In the upper half, hard, gleaming steel pipes reach into the empty sky. Through the subterranean application of industrial technology then, CRA thrusts up into the light and space above the surface of the planet on which we all live.

Even though this was an advertisement for a transnational mining company, it was speaking a language common to most Australians. In the 1950s and 1960s, even critics as wary of big capitalism as Clem Christensen still felt that we had a moral obligation to embrace the ideals of globalised industrial development. As Christensen said, library stock should be 'leaping to keep pace' with all other aspects of the nation's 'phenomenal development'. Such assertions were all in a good cause, as Christensen was seriously concerned that intellectualism not be displaced by philistinism, and that material prosperity be partnered by knowledge and education, not simply as adjuncts either, but as ends in themselves.

At the same time, Christensen ends up having to express these sentiments in the very same language as the digger-uppers and the cutters-down and all the other unrestrained exploiters. This is disappointing, though understandable, because this language was both infectious and effective. For example, even George Johnston's semi-autobiographical hero David Meredith, usually a stridently bohemian critic of Australian provincialism and materialism, buys into the dream of development in *Clean Straw for Nothing* (1969), the sequel to *My Brother Jack* (1964). This is how he describes the orgasmic celebration of progress that is the Snowy Mountains Scheme to his wife Cressida:

The yellow tractors against the glaring drifts of snow, the beards and mackinaws, the polyglot babble of smoke-hazed mess huts, the tingling atmosphere of a collective excitement . . . 'It's like coming to an oasis in a desert, when you've been thirsting for something of promise, something to believe in. It's magnificent darling! It's exciting! It's the only *visionary* thing I've seen since I've been back in this bloody country. It's the most fabulous theme. It's got everything. *Everything!*'[116]

Johnston's rich imagery of the utopian possibilities of industrial development provides a textual synthesis of the industrial and the cultural in much the same manner as the CRA advertisement draws *Meanjin* and the mining corporation together. And it isn't hard to understand why such Australian intellectuals, normally reticent when it came to the operations of big business, were excited by the ideal of development. For a hundred and eighty years after all, European Australians had been hacking away at the landscape with an almost boundless enthusiasm, so much so that it had come to seem one's basic moral duty. At the micro level, as Nino Culotta put it, 'whenever I had a fiver I bought something, and whenever I had a weekend I built something'.[117] On the macro level, as CRA's marketing department saw it, it was the task of companies like CRA and journals like *Meanjin* to provide the means whereby 'both industry and the arts can enrich the life of our community'.[118] While Clem Christensen may not have seen the relationship as quite so cosy, or put it in quite the same terms, other advertisements placed in *Meanjin* by the other industrial giants of the 1960s, like Shell and BHP and, as previously noted, GMH, couched their appeals in the same fashion, and in the end for *Meanjin* what mattered most was that they brought in cash, and this kept the journal and its intellectual project alive.

There may be a case to be made that all this was only the rhetoric of advertisers, and that we shouldn't perhaps take it so seriously. I would, however, emphasise that these advertisements are intended to make sense, not nonsense, and they make their sense in a specific cultural context. As Deleuze and Guattari note in *A Thousand Plateaus*, anyone 'can shout "I declare a general mobilization," but in the absence of an effectuated variable giving that person the right to make such a statement it is an act of puerility or insanity, not an act of enunciation'.[119] And so, if we have a close look at this particular issue of *Meanjin*, we can see on every page sense being made, though it is always being made in the parlance and the values of the times. Literary critics seek to penetrate texts in order to uncover their riches, while miners seek to do the same thing to the landscape, and so life back then went on. But, we still need to remember that as with all acts of violence, whether textual or industrial, somebody always gets hurt.

In the early 1960s, while Conzinc Riotinto's marketers were, like Wynn's, organising the placement of advertisements in the literary journals enjoyed by James Halliday, the main industrial focus of the company was a number of large mining projects across the nation. The smelting of lead at Port Pirie in South Australia, the extraction of iron ore from the Pilbara in Western Australia, and the mining of uranium at Rum Jungle in the Northern Territory and at Mary Kathleen in Queensland were CRA's biggest profit generators and most high-profile operations, while the company was also investing heavily in the development of bauxite mines in western Cape York. In *Taming the Great South Land*, a unique narrative of the exploitation of the Australian landmass following European occupation, William J. Lines gives an account of the commencement of the Cape York operations. Lines details how in 1957 the Queensland government,

> awarded Comalco (a consortium of Conzinc Riotinto Australia [CRA], a subsidiary of Rio Tinto Zinc [RTZ] of London, and British Aluminium, and later, the United States based Kaiser Aluminium) mining rights for bauxite over 5800 square kilometres of land on the Aboriginal reserves of Weipa, Mapoon and Aurukun on Cape York Peninsula – the largest reserves of Aboriginal land in eastern Australia. Comalco obtained an

84-year lease over the area at royalties of five to ten cents a ton – the
cheapest in the world. To remove the bauxite, Comalco planned to bull-
doze 230 centimetres of topsoil, then rip out the six or so metres of
ore-bearing clay from the land over hundreds of square kilometres.[120]

There was, however, one problem: the traditional owners of the land,
having lived in the area for countless generations, were reluctant to
move. This issue was dealt with in November 1963, in a manner
familiar enough in Queensland, when police under instructions from
the Queensland Director of Aboriginal Affairs arrived at Mapoon by
boat, burnt down the buildings, and rounded everyone up. As one
former resident, Rachel Peter, tells it:

> People don't know how we were treated. They destroyed the homes,
> burnt them down you know. And I seen all the burning down of the
> homes, the church . . . It was destroying our culture, our lives. You
> know the land is part of our lives. I said, you know, you destroyed
> everything from us . . . [121]

The families were forced 150 kilometres north to Bamaga, where a
new settlement was built for them and they were dumped down to
start their lives again. There was little chance of the confrontation
being played out any other way. As the Army's faux nuking of central
Cape York showed, there wasn't a lot of respect down south for either
the landscape or for any of the people who lived on and in it. And
especially not when there was money to be made. As Lines notes,
Comalco 'received Aboriginal land containing $60 million worth of
bauxite', while Weipa became 'the biggest bauxite exporting port in
the world'.[122] This was the way it went in Queensland, as in much
of the country. By the end of the decade the Sunshine State's mines
minister, 'Big' Ernie Evans, would be a partner with the Premier Joh
Bjelke-Petersen in an oil exploration company.[123]

In such a climate the violently disrupted lives of the people of
Mapoon amounted to collateral damage (as the Americans would
later come to call it), in the global struggle for markets, profits and

military dominance. Moreover, these factors are particularly crucial here, as aluminium was as vital to American military aircraft production at this high point of the Cold War as it was to the American-dominated civilian airliner industry. But the uses of the bauxite, and the consequences of its extraction, were barely noticed footnotes to what appeared at the time as the main game: Australia's resources boom and the celebration of national development that it generated. Far away from Cape York, in New South Wales, a school textbook from the time told the story of the expulsion of the residents of Mapoon this way:

> In North Queensland, the largest and finest deposits of bauxite in the world were discovered in 1955. Located at Weipa, the deposits are easily mined and shipped to refineries at Gladstone in Queensland and Bell Bay in Tasmania or exported to Japan and Europe . . . Aluminium is an extremely valuable metal for modern industries.[124]

In just such ways was *terra nullius* still finding its way into the textual fabric of the Australian nation, even in the 1960s. And yet the impact of the European occupation of the continent on the lives of Indigenous Australians and their displacement to the peripheries of the nation – the edges of towns, the remote regions of states, the verges of the economy and of mainstream cultural life – haunted the collective unconscious of progress-fixated White Australia at every step. Indeed, there is a perfect example of the power of this haunting in the March 1964 issue of *Meanjin*, in the short story 'The Man Who was Different' by John Bellair.

The story's setting is a cattle drive somewhere in central Australia and the two principal characters are Arthur, a 'young half-caste', and Alec, a white novice jackeroo from the city. These two are constantly rubbing each other up the wrong way, and eventually have a punch-up in which Arthur fights 'savagely', his aim being to 'kill Alec'. Alec nonetheless wins, while Arthur, slumped on the ground, put his head on his arm and sobbed as though his heart would break. Alec, shaking and gasping, stood and watched in amazement. When Arthur's sobs turned to steady blubbing, Alec in pity walked away and flung himself on his back beside his swag.

He got up after a while, rinsed his mouth and drank some water. Arthur was still lying there. He took the water Alec brought him. Whatever devil had been in him had gone. . .

From that time Arthur became Alec's devoted slave. You could not describe it in any other way. Alec, at first embarrassed when Arthur gathered buck-bush to put under his campsheet, accepted it because there seemed to be nothing else to do. And the next day he found his saddle-cloth washed. When Syd took over the cooking again, Arthur would ask Alec each morning what horse he wanted and would saddle it for him.[125]

The narrative is then reconciled when Arthur 'goes walkabout', thus finally defusing the residue of discomfort left from Alec's victory. 'The Man Who was Different' is an exceedingly depressing text whichever way you look at it. Is the half-caste (to use the racist descriptor then current) Arthur a cipher for Indigenous Australians in general, the violent struggle in which he engages with Alec emblematic of Aboriginal resistance? Or is he just a projection of a white fantasy of conquest and subjugation? Either way, the servile groveling he engages in after losing the fight simply reads now as a pathetic piece of racist jingoism. Alec, European and rational, is 'embarrassed' at the turn of events. The primitive Arthur meanwhile loses his irrationality, and therefore his independence, once the there is no more 'devil' in him. And how does the story conclude? With Arthur leaving of course. From a colonialist point of view this is the preferred ending: if only *they* would just go away, then *we* could have the country all to ourselves. A few years after this story was written, I remember my primary school teacher, a gentle young woman who used to play us The Seekers' *Morningtown Ride* and get us to sing along, telling me and my impressionable classmates that 'when we grew up' we 'wouldn't have to worry about Aborigines', because by then, they would have all 'died out'.

Again, such discordance within the body of the nation was papered over by texts such as CRA's advertisements in *Meanjin*. According to CRA, the goals of the transnational miner and the goals of *Meanjin* were one: to enrich the life of our community, a nation united as one in the common cause of industrial development. But, as Benedict Anderson demonstrates in *Imagined Communities*, such a conception of communality can only ever be a fiction.[126] In a society with a massively unequal distribution of power, wealth and knowledge, the idea of a homogeneous national purpose is wholly mythical. Yet the knights of the realm who made up the Menzies Government in the 1950s and 60s expended much of their hot air insisting that we were lucky to live in a free, classless society.

There is an essay by Walter Benjamin called 'Eduard Fuchs, Historian and Collector' (1937), and it contains one my favourites of his countless remarkable observations. That it is also one of his most oft-quoted lines is at least some kind of testament to its power. 'There is', Benjamin writes, 'no document of culture which is not at the same time a document of barbarism'.[127] A contemporary of Benjamin's, Fuchs was a German cultural historian and collector of caricatures, lithographs and erotica – minor, ephemeral or 'low' works which, so Benjamin argues, constituted an alternative conception of art: an art of the ordinary, not of the exalted old masters.

This is why Benjamin was interested in Eduard Fuchs. For Fuchs, anonymous sculptures from the T'ang period in China, for example, provided an illumination, not of the experience of an individual artist, but of 'the way in which the world and things are grasped as a whole'.[128] In stating that a work of culture is always a record of barbarism, Benjamin was applying such anti-individualist sentiments to the problem of contemporary culture, which for him, was in the last instance always grounded in the atrocity of exclusion. As Benjamin saw it, for every successful, influential text of culture there are countless other texts, the stories of other experiences, other lives, that are never seen, never heard, never known. Our culture values and reproduces the experiences of certain individuals only, which become the official historical and cultural record, while the 'anonymous toil of their contemporaries' disappears without trace.[129]

Inspired by such ideas, I'd argue that it would be difficult to find a more appropriate example of the barbarism of a cultural document, a document of *our* culture, than CRA's advertisement in the March 1964 *Meanjin*. A celebration of the drive to 'uncover the hidden potential', it is a document that simultaneously covers up the space in which a group of people were forced crying onto a boat as their home was destroyed and everything they'd known and loved all their lives was taken away from them.[130] It is a document obliterating the fact that these people who had *failed to penetrate* and *failed to uncover hidden potential* received no compensation from the companies and the government that ripped what had been their land to pieces, turning the much-desired red earth into aircraft for America's expanding war against North Vietnam, and into aluminium foil for the shelves of Australian's pantries while channeling the profits generated to corporate headquarters in Europe and North America. This is the alternate story of Mapoon, a place like all the other places across our nation where not only land but also much more was lost, where people were shot and stabbed and clubbed and poisoned and starved. This is, in the end, the story of how this particular place became another, very different place.

The advertisement run in *Meanjin* by CRA effaces the story of what happened at Mapoon. CRA's advert and its placement draws the journal's readers toward an imagined community of fellow members sharing similar goals, and working towards the same end: enriching the life of *our* community. In reality, and to reverse John Howard's dictum of 'for all of us', this can only ever be a community for some of us. Similarly, Wynn's invitation to all those who appreciated 'a good red wine' draws together a similar group, those who could take a quiet sip, sit back and turn the page, and contemplate the literary life, while other people guzzled down beer and had to use, in Nino Culotta's words, the sweat of their head to earn their crust.

Despite the fact that he proved to be one of the twentieth century's greatest exponents of the genre, Walter Benjamin was pessimistic about the project of a cultural history. He felt that no matter what object the historian or analyst looked upon, such objects were merely the product of a historical descent that one could not 'observe without horror'.[131] For Benjamin, writing in 1937, the search for an all-encompassing cultural history that could tell the whole story, a story that would include all the exclusions as well as all the consecrated histories, all the Mapoons as much as all the mining industry triumphs, was by its very nature impossible.

Benjamin was probably right, and he never came near to finishing his 'Arcades Project' because he wanted to write a work that was about everything, a book that had everything in it. His subsequent failure to produce such an all-encompassing work was in fact the whole point, as Benjamin knew better than anyone. It is, after all, only in the minor and the partial histories that the otherwise silenced voices find a space. It is only in the close-up, rather than the panorama, that the moments of barbarism and pain are brought to light.

6. The Men of Courage

Outside the main entrance to Roselands shopping centre in south-west Sydney is a heritage panel explaining the historical significance of the place. One of a number of such panels placed in various locations across the Canterbury City Council district by the local historical society, it tells us that this was once the site of Belmore House, a local manor, and displays two photographs: the house as it was in the 1880s, and its owner, a former steam tug operator turned farmer. The story continues: in 1942 Belmore House was taken over by the Army, and in 1943 the local mayor bought it and established a market garden, and after the war he turned it into a golf course, which he called Roselands. According to the last sentence on the panel, Grace Brothers then bought the land and Roselands, the shopping centre, opened in 1965.

For the cultural historian this information panel creates a vague sense of anxiety. Here, at one of the most significant sites of the many that make up the history of consumerism in Australia, all we find is a scratchy, grainy image of an old house alongside a small portrait of a white man with a beard. Here, where if anywhere you might expect to find some trace, some public record of the currents and forces shaping modern experience, there is only the same old story: men and property. Look away from the panel and you'll see that the other story, that of Australia's first large-scale enclosed shopping mall, is right in front of you, all glass and tile and concrete. As its absence from the information panel demonstrates though, it isn't the sort of story that historical societies much care for. After all, how can a chronicle of air-conditioning and car parking, of fashion parades and take-away food constitute history? There are no individual stories to research, no faded images to unearth, no single owner or originator to ascribe existence to. And so the information panel ignores this story, instead telling anyone who cares to look at it that John Fenwick once had a house on this spot. Meanwhile, people bustle past it while others stand around oblivious, waiting for buses, catching cabs, meeting friends and lovers, sitting on benches, just as they have done every day since Roselands opened in 1965.

Drawing on the language of advertising, we can say that Roselands was much more than just a shopping centre. And really, this is quite true, it was much more, it was a major cultural event, a major turning point in the history of consumerism in Australia. And, if we wanted to periodise the place in terms of cultural theory, we could also say its opening was a key moment in the experience of late modernity in Australia. But how can such assertions be justified, you may ask? After all, Roselands was, still is, only a shopping centre. True, but in the 1960s Roselands was said to be the biggest shopping centre 'in the southern hemisphere'.[132] This trite phrase had high currency in Australia in the 1960s. It consistently affirmed our status as successful antipodean battlers, never expecting to eclipse the achievements of Europe or, more importantly, North America, but confirming that, unlike the majority of our hemisphere's inhabitants, we were at least in the game.

The currency of antipodean bigness bestowed a cringing sense of self-worth, usually to the point of banality. As former Labor politician Lindsay Tanner recalls, when he was a boy in Melbourne he often used to walk past a giant hole in the ground in Brunswick. It was the Brunswick tip, which many proud locals would tell him was the biggest such hole in the ground in the southern hemisphere.[133] Roselands, however, was said to be the biggest shopping centre in the southern hemisphere, and this, at a time when consumerism as a mode of social organisation was becoming the predominant cultural form across much of the globe, was something to celebrate. If even a hole in the ground was a thing to be proud of, then an ultra modern shopping centre was surely nothing less than deliriously exciting.

The Biggest Shopping Centre in the Southern Hemisphere was then a marker that clearly identified Roselands in the nationalist and developmentalist terms of the day: if it was big then it was obviously important, just as it was obviously important because it was big. As well as a celebration of consumer culture, Roselands was also very much a celebration of the modernist ideals of unity, homogeneity and totality, and of the promise of social order brought about by the unrestrained application of technology. It was an affirmation, too, of the seemingly limitless potential of the economies of the West during the long postwar boom, when the prospect of continuous economic growth seemed as solid as the concrete that gave it form. And this is why Roselands was much more than just a shopping centre. It was very much a part of the political and economic narrative of the West, and in this sense it was a geo-political space as much as a social and cultural space.

Roselands was also a media event, at a time in Australia when metropolitan media were at last becoming comprehensive enough (morning and afternoon daily newspapers, radio and television, fed by the expanding public relations and marketing industry) to be able to generate such events. Consequently, it had become a regular feature of the Sydney press long before it opened. From the time excavation began on the site of the former golf course, the metropolitan newspapers ran stories on the works in progress. A *Daily Telegraph* series that began with a hole in the ground in February 1964 reported in September 1965 that 'it had to come – a space age shopping centre', the 'centre of the future'.[134] Life, so the *Telegraph* said, would never be the same again, while the *Daily Mirror* claimed that Roselands ensured 'shopping will no longer be a boring chore . . . it will out-mode shopping as we know it and lead to a new way of life for thousands'.[135] The other afternoon newspaper, the *Sun*, quoted Pat Primmer aged 20 of Punchbowl, a store guide, who thought that the complex was just 'so new, so modern, so . . . so exciting'.[136]

Robert Askin, Premier of New South Wales, presided over the official opening at 3pm on 11 October 1965. Askin was conscious, in his way, of the historical significance of the moment. The 'million dollar spread of merchandise under this roof', he told the audience, 'brings the city to the suburbs in a glittering way that must rival even the fabled Persian Bazaars.'[137] Such orientalist observations are of course the hallmark of provincialism, a point perfectly illustrated a century earlier by Homais the pharmacist in *Madame Bovary* who, overcome by the excitement of the town's agricultural show day, imagines that his 'little locality could have fancied itself transported into the midst of a scene from the Thousand and One Nights'.[138] And for that matter, one could also point to Bill Buckley's comparison of the St George Leagues Club to the Taj Mahal. Anyway, flushed with excitement over the dual celebration of capitalism and industrial development that was Roselands, Askin declared it 'symptomatic of a new and exciting era of expansion . . . a great adventure by private enterprise to meet the challenge of providing the shopping public of New South Wales with the most modern facilities'. Three thousand guests listened to the speech and watched the unveiling of a plaque commemorating the event in the centre court of what was, to date, by far the most ambitious shopping centre to have been built in Australia.

Publicity material issued by the developers, Grace Brothers, stressed the details of the centre's physical form: the 'countless feats

of engineering skill', the overall size of the project, the 26,500 flo-
rescent tubes in the lighting system, and the 847 loudspeakers in the
public address systems.[139] The construction was claimed as a record
by Grace Brothers for the fastest piece of building work in Australian
industrial history. 'I have never seen such enthusiastic workmen, they
are really living this project', said the Roselands property manager.[140]
A full-page newspaper advertisement for Roselands featured a map
showing the centre's precise position in relation to the rest of Sydney:
from now on 'all roads lead to Roselands'.[141] On the first day of trad-
ing it was estimated that between 30,000 and 70,000 people visited
from 6 a.m. onwards even though the shops didn't open until nine.

The technical and industrial developments of American-centred
globalised capitalism, which during the 1950s and 60s in Australia
manifested most clearly in the form of streamlined Holdens and
Fords, were now embodied in a large privately controlled public
space. Yet if Roselands did represent a change, it was not in the production of consumer goods, but rather in their delivery. Its opening
didn't mean that there was an immediate increase in the range of
products available for consumers, nor did those consumers suddenly
have more money to spend. Rather, access to shops had now been
dramatically rearranged so that, instead of having to deal with the
expansive strip of a suburban main street, the shopper now browsed
within a concentrated indoor space. This meant, so it was claimed,
that shopping was turned from a laborious task that the housewife
(typically) was obliged to perform into a pleasure that she, or indeed
anyone, was now able to enjoy. This would have a dramatic, transformative resonance, and to an extent the effusive *Daily Telegraph*
was correct to assert that life would 'never be the same again'. Even
the antiquarian Prime Minister, a few months away from retirement,
had noticed that the ground had shifted. Addressing the Australian
Advertisers Association the same day that Roselands opened, Sir

Robert observed that it was 'obvious' that 'effective advertising had become a vital element in private enterprise', adding that 'in today's world it was no longer possible to rely on the efforts of the door-to-door salesman'.[142]

On the Sunday before the official opening the *Sun-Herald* carried ten consecutive pages of architectural sketches, photographs, advertisements, headlines and stories on the 'garden city in the suburbs', telling its readers that 'Tuesday will bring the dawn of a new way of life for you, your family, your friends. ROSELANDS . . . makes its glorious debut'.[143] On the following day the *Sydney Morning Herald*, the *Daily Telegraph*, the *Sun*, and the *Daily Mirror* all carried supplements of between ten and twenty pages, combining journalists' copy with Grace Brothers' publicity blurbs in expansive advertorials. The *Herald*, departing from the anti-populist style that usually defined it against both its tabloid competition and Fairfax's own *Sun*, began its coverage with the statement that 'the visitor's first reaction is to wonder . . . at the sort of courage that was needed to sink six million pounds into a spot by-passed by commerce about half-way between Hurstville and Bankstown'. Just like the men who built the Taj Mahal in Kogarah, the men who ran Grace Brothers were also self-made men who got things done, who turned holes in the ground into suburban palaces. Apparently, creating Roselands had been a courageous act, and one needed to show 'respect for the men who had the necessary courage'.[144] Another article, perhaps providing Premier Askin with his cue, told of how 'The Centre Court is the pulse of Roselands, capturing as it does the colour and excitement, the lure and bustle of a bazaar in a twentieth-century setting'.[145]

According to the *Sydney Morning Herald*, Roselands was 'in some important ways more advanced than anything in the United States', a result of the fact that Whitehead and Payne, the Sydney architectural firm that designed Roselands, had previously created a prototype enclosed shopping centre, Monaro Mall, in Canberra. And now they had studied the standard American shopping mall design and decided that 'the American conception could be bettered'. This 'city in the suburbs' which Whitehead and Payne visualised 'need not sprawl', it could and would 'be a compacted, three level, weatherproof, air-conditioned "town" between walls'.[146] Similarly, the *Sun-Herald* claimed that Roselands' design was 'a complete departure from the American-pattern regional centre',[147] while the *Daily Telegraph* gave an account of Grace Brothers senior staff making 'frequent world-wide study tours . . . to anticipate developments in merchandise presentation'.[148]

Perhaps there were some ways in which Roselands could be seen as differing from anything built in the United States, but mostly it was remarkably similar to the American model. Roselands embodied a basic structure first used in the Southdale complex in Minneapolis in 1956, a design that was celebrated in sections of the North American media in a similar manner to that of Roselands in Sydney, a design which John Casazza and Frank Spink, authors of the *Shopping Centre Development Handbook,* point out was to become 'the dominant building form for regional centers by the 1960s'.[149] Nor was Roselands even the first enclosed shopping centre built in Sydney, as centres at both Chatswood and Miranda, opened in 1963 and 1964 respectively, had also taken this form though Roselands was of course much bigger.

If there was one major difference between Roselands and the standard American shopping mall like Southdale, then this concerned the centre's car park rather than the design of its central concourse. Due to a lack of space at the site (strictly limited to the area of the old golf course), most of Roselands' parking area was provided by a decked car park attached to the western side of the building. This was a distinct departure from comparable American regional shopping centres, located either in developing urban areas or on the edge of existing outer suburbs and typically surrounded by open, single-level parking. Roselands had instead been placed on a finite space in the middle of suburbs created during the 1930s. It was therefore the decked car park that was the truly inventive feature of Roselands, a fitting piece of innovation in a nation that was rapidly becoming one of the world's most car-dependent societies. But who would want to split such hairs when national pride was involved? So, the emotive signifiers 'new development' and 'best in the world' came to define not just the car park, but Roselands as a whole.

Another key feature of Roselands as a Sydney media event was the amount of attention paid to the selection by aerial survey of a location for the centre, a spot 'somewhere' in the 'sprawling southwest of Sydney', as it was described. This was Roselands' own foundation myth, and it echoed the foundation myth of the nation itself, established on an unknown (to Europeans) continental coast 'discovered' in 1770 by Captain Cook. Similarly, the land that would be Roselands lay undiscovered in the sprawling suburbs until the day the men of courage singled out its location on their map, at the point where commerce and history converged.

Celebrating the new technologies given form in Roselands, a *Sunday Telegraph* article had Grace Brothers operatives hovering over the suburbs of the Canterbury district in a helicopter as they searched for a suitable spot, though given this was Australia in 1956, the *Sydney Morning Herald*'s detailed account two days later of an 'architect and a photographer shuttling to and fro' in a propeller-driven Tiger Moth biplane is likely to be more accurate.[150] The image of the helicopter equated with the 'space-age shopping centre', while the Tiger Moth certainly didn't – it was a clunky throwback to the early years of the century. Yet the type of aircraft used was also less important than the actual practice itself, aerial surveillance, a century-old mapping technique that had reached a peak of refinement in the Second World War as an aid to the area bombing of enemy cities and the industries and civilian populations contained therein. Now aerial surveillance was being used for the far more benign job of market spotting.

Roselands, as it emerges from these newspaper articles, really was an embodiment of the postwar technological revolution. By all accounts it was a technical success of the highest order, and the particular forms of spatial and social order that constituted the shopping centre as a public space were at all times interpreted by the Sydney media within a modernist framework of technological triumphalism. As the store guide Pat from Punchbowl said, sounding just like one of the characters from a groovy cosmopolitan film like John Schlesinger's *Darling* (1965), it was all so new, so modern and so exciting.

New, modern and *exciting*: the three key concepts underpinning the mushrooming consumer world. Yet despite the centrality of consumption to the Roselands enterprise, the centre attempted to provide much more than just a new, modern and exciting shopping experience. In sanctioning the project, Canterbury Council had also stipulated that Roselands be *much more than just a shopping centre*, that it should in fact be a shopping-community centre. To this end, the rose gardens that had been a landscape feature of the golf course (providing its name) were retained within the borders of the site, as was a lawn bowls club, while attempts were made by Grace Brothers to interact with the local community in more ways than just shopping. At Kingsgrove North High School, for example, a young George Gittoes won a painting competition sponsored by the nearby development. Ironically, for Gittoes this was the start of a career representing the lives of working-class people rather than one celebrating the glories of capitalism and consumerism.[151]

The communitarian aspects of the centre weren't just on the outside, they were built into its very fabric and form. Again, due

127

to Canterbury Council requirements, Roselands included a public library. It also contained child-care facilities, augmented by a unique observational system called the 'TV Child Minder':

> The most unusual feature of the child-minding centre at Roselands is the automatic closed-circuit television system which will 'report' to parents on screens throughout the centre.
>
> The TV system will end the worries of parents who feel uneasy about leaving their children with strangers, or worry about them fretting . . .
>
> The closed-circuit television is the largest in Australia.[152]

And, indeed, Roselands was full of strategically placed television monitors displaying grainy black-and-white images of the goings-on within the creche, which the newly technologically liberated young mums were free to glance up at any time they wished, so as to be able to simultaneously shop and monitor their youngsters. It was of course touted as the biggest such surveillance system in Australia, though significantly not the southern hemisphere, as the surveillance systems of the racist government of South Africa, or maybe those of the American-backed military dictatorship that ruled Brazil, had probably taken the title in that field. Anyway, as with many other aspects of Roselands, this state-of-the-art child-care service was a prescient harbinger of the massive expansion and permeation of surveillance and control technologies within industrial societies over the next few decades. At this time though, in order to access it you had to go shopping at Roselands.[153]

But maybe we are getting a little carried away here with the majesty that was Roselands. While the Biggest Shopping Centre in the Southern Hemisphere *was* a major event, I wouldn't want to give the impression that this was the only story in the Sydney press at the time. Naturally it wasn't. For example, Roselands coincided with the Indonesian military's operations to purge the nation of communists and leftists in the wake of a failed officers' coup against the Sukarno

Government. On the day Roselands opened, the *Daily Mirror* was reporting on an 'Indo Mob's Anger', detailing how 'enraged mobs in Djakarta yesterday sacked the Communist Headquarters and burned down the home of the party's leader'.[154] This was the start of a campaign of disinformation, repression and murder by the Indonesian armed forces that would result in the deaths of at least half a million people as Suharto's New Order regime took power in Australia's closest neighbour, a nation whose seemingly outlandish name the *Daily Mirror* subeditors couldn't even be bothered to articulate in full, even as they ejaculated with praise over a bunch of suburban shops.

In regards to another front, the *Sun-Herald* of 10 October 1965 was relating with obscene detachment the detail of 'How Hanoi Rides the US Blitz':

> Johns coming, Johns coming yell the little North Vietnamese children as they scurry through the country lanes and city streets. John to them stands for Johnson and it's their way of announcing to their neighbours that the U.S. Air Force is coming over again with its shrieking silver jets.[155]

Every day, as the newly liberated suburban consumers of Sydney made their way through the maze of shops sitting atop the old Roselands golf course, American bombers were attacking the people of North Vietnam. In March 1965 'John', US President Lyndon Johnson, had launched his 'Rolling Thunder' bombing campaign, designed to cower the Vietnamese communists into surrendering. This, though, was an application of new technologies that left most Australians largely unaffected in their daily experience, apart from one exception: the air defence exercise over Sydney the night after Roselands opened, in which a group of American jet fighters attempted a mock attack on the city while the Royal Australian Air Force practised repelling them. The next day the *Sydney Morning Herald* reported that the planes 'woke babies, angered old people and frightened a good proportion of Sydney's population'. An RAAF spokesman replied to the criticism with the terse assertion that freedom had to be paid for, one way or another: 'This is the price of defence in today's supersonic age. We will have to get used to it.'[156] It was a simple proposition. If we wanted to be free to shop, then we had to put up with being terrorised occasionally by the sharp end of the military-industrial complex. Because, as John Updike's naive but cynical alter ego 'Rabbit' Angstrom would imagine a few years later: 'paradise' was indeed 'possible' beneath America's 'patient bombers'.[157]

But the pretend air attack was an interruption of everyday life in Sydney, not the norm, as it was in the towns and villages of North Vietnam. Nor did the planes drop any bombs or wreak any carnage. They just woke people up. In Sydney, most of the time, the supersonic age was far more tangible in Roselands' benign applications of the new technology. It was evident in Australia's largest closed-circuit television and air-conditioning systems, but its most dramatic manifestation was the Raindrop Fountain in the centre court. This 'grand spectacle' was composed of 'one hundred and fifty miles of nylon thread' and 'vivid green shrubbery and pink tiling', and was designed 'to create the illusion of fine mist on lush foliage in a stunning, steamy jungle backdrop'.[158] As with many aspects of Roselands' physical form, the newspapers were full of details as to what made the fountain tick: the nylon threads were spaced three-quarters of an inch (1.9 centimetres) apart; they formed the outline of a raindrop screen 47 feet (13.7 metres) in circumference; they were set into a base 3 feet (0.9 metres) below the floor and rose 30 feet (9 metres) to the ceiling, and all the while subtle lighting played on a specially designed fluid sliding down in droplets over the hundreds of threads creating the 'illusion of a continual downpour'.[159]

It is probably overstating the obvious to point out that as public art the Raindrop Fountain, with its soft pink and green tones, was the ultimate in 1960s kitsch. As a fountain it was an extreme parody of the bubbling fixtures found in the town squares of Europe. You couldn't drink the special fluid and the throwing of coins wasn't encouraged. Yet as a spectacle it was absolute affect, and as such it held the shopping centre together as a technological and social space. Roselands might have been all artifice, but its artificiality definitely pointed the way to the future. Indeed, it *was* the future, and the absolutely unnatural Raindrop Fountain indicated that a new, technology-based reality was displacing the old unruly world of uncontrolled natural elements. In the end it may have been junk but, like the other elements of 1960s psychedelia to which it was related, it was very affecting junk.

*

In *The Language of Post-Modern Architecture*, Charles Jencks outlines what he calls the modernist faith in the 'heroism of everyday life'. For Jencks, this was a failed dream, as the reformism of modernist artists and architects in the first half of the twentieth century, with their plans to reinvigorate democratic society via the veneration of everyday objects and the creation of a new class of social technicians and managers, soured as the century wore on. Then, 'the dream was taken over by Madison Avenue (and its equivalents),' and 'the heroic object of everyday use' became the 'new, revolutionary detergent'.[160]

Jencks' account of the 'takeover of the dream' and the rise of a banal form of consumerism is incisive, though it is also underpinned by just the sort of modernist logic he is attempting to criticise. For Jencks is working with what could be termed the notion of the 'pre-cultural object'. That is to say, an implicit valuation of consumer goods which divides them into essential objects, the 'desire' for which can be rationally explained, and a mass of inessential ones, like the new 'revolutionary' detergent, the product of the regime of advertising.[161] Not surprisingly, it is the point of view held by the (usually white, middle-class, male) cultural critic that determines whether the consumer item in question is worthy or unworthy, largely on the basis of whether it is significant or not for him.

As Meaghan Morris argues in her influential essay 'Things To Do with Shopping Centres', another way to look at consumer society is to refuse this binary division of good and bad, worthy and unworthy, and to try to understand the products on offer in the society of mass consumption as amounting to no less than a 'lived aesthetic', an array, in other words, of socially produced, culturally constituted objects in economic circulation.[162] Looked at from this point of view, Roselands was as much a place to experience the society of consumption as it was simply a place to consume. Maybe another story that ran in the *Sun-Herald* that Sunday, 10 October 1965, can help illustrate this last argument. Headlined 'The Soup Can Artist', the article gives an account of the activities of Andy Warhol, the New York artist who was 'the most outrageous thing in culture', according to the newspaper, 'since Dali':

> A typical Warhol painting has no limp watches or dead horses, but simply an only too familiar can of soup repeated 120 times on an eight-by-six foot canvas.
>
> His soup tins with their glorification of the banal spawned a whole school of supermarket art which focuses on household foods and brand names.
>
> Warhol's current artworks are silk screen reproductions . . .
>
> He has not touched a paint-brush since he gave up his job as a commercial artist drawing shoes for advertisements.[163]

While Warhol's Campbell's soup can paintings had been seen as avant-garde in the United States in the early 1960s (being bought up, for example, by young nonconformists like the Californian actor Dennis Hopper), by the mid-sixties he'd moved on to films, such as the minimalist epic *Empire*, a static eight-hour study of the Empire State Building, which was also mentioned in the article. The Warhol of this period has generally been defined in one of three ways. Ideally, he was the hero of everyday life: 'he made us feel that even in the simplest of commodities and the most commonplace of subjects there was a great deal of poetry and meaning.'[164] Alternatively, he was a critic of consumerism, the producer of 'a pulp-derived, bleakly monochrome vision that held, however tenuous the grip, to an all-but-buried tradition of truth-telling in American commercial culture.'[165] Or, he was simply a cynical opportunist: 'how could otherwise informed people in the sixties and seventies imagine that the man who would end up running a gossip magazine . . . for a living was really a cultural subversive?'[166] Of course, from a postmodern point of view all of these interpretations are probably correct. Yet Warhol's own statement about the object repetition paintings perhaps comes closest to an explanation of their 'meaning': 'I just paint those objects in my paintings because those are the things I know best . . . I feel very much a part of my times, of my culture, as much a part of it as rocket ships and television.'[167]

In Australia, mass consumption was also now a way of life, and the appearance of this profile of the 'soup can artist' in the Sydney press the day before the opening of Roselands announces a statement similar to Warhol's own. He and his work were just simply a part of American culture, which was now our culture. The soup can, a metonym of everyday consumption, is in the right place at the right time, with the newspaper providing both a form and a format for talking about not just Warhol, but about the entire lived aesthetic of consumerism. Understanding that consuming had become a 'way of life', and writing in response to the appearance of the first enclosed shopping malls in France in the late 1960s, Jean Baudrillard detailed the realities of this new, dominating aesthetic, arguing that at 'the heart of consumption' is 'the total organization of everyday life . . . a complete homogenization', with consumption 'a collective and active behaviour, a constraint, a morality, and an institution. It is a complete system of values, with all that the term implies concerning group integration and social control'.[168]

With hindsight we can see that the system of consumerism is not as complete as the totalising rhetoric of Baudrillard would have us believe. Consumers aren't passive, and we don't buy everything that's put in front of us. At the same time though, a key effect of the mega-mall phenomenon has indeed been the partial masking of difference and contradiction within social life, and the displacement of the manifold problems inherent in a society based on varying levels of greed and exploitation by the image of a world in which everything was buyable and everything was climate-controlled. For readers of the *Sun-Herald* in October 1965, the ideological transference from the consumable to the site of the ultimate consumer experience was, potentially, achieved merely by turning the page of the newspaper and moving on from Warhol's depiction of soup cans to the place where you could buy cans of soup.

> ROSELANDS has EVERYTHING the people need . . . But, that's not all, no matter what the weather outside, once you step inside ROSELANDS the huge all-enclosed Shopping Community area is climate-controlled to the temperature of a pleasant Spring day, all year through.

This piece of advertorialism writes Roselands as much more than just a place to do some shopping, it is a celebration of the modernist project of management and control, of the techno-industrial dream of a society in which the people have everything they need, provided for by an economic order of truly global proportions. According to the *Sydney Morning Herald*, Roselands had 'all the amenities of a city'. And as the newspaper observed without comment, it had 'practically everything except a church', an interesting admission in itself in terms of the cultural unconscious and one that spoke volumes about the way shopping was fast becoming the secular religion of godless, global consumer society.[169]

As sites of consumption, the direct antecedents of Roselands are most obviously the great bourgeois department stores of the nineteenth century, though in a complementary fashion Roselands, as an ideological space, can also be seen to derive from the international exhibitions and world's fairs held in the European capitals and North American cities from the 1850s onwards. As Paul Greenhalgh put in *Ephemeral Vistas*:

> Technology would transform the world, bring plenty, peace, unity, all in the foreseeable future. Such beliefs were stated in twentieth-century exhibitions more often than in their earlier counterparts, but from the Great Exhibition onwards the machine was consistently presented as the Messiah which would lead the human race to the Promised Land . . .
>
> As cultural manifestations, they revealed an expansive West in its most flamboyant and bombastic state; baroque, overblown expressions of societies that felt they ruled the material world absolutely.[170]

The New York World's Fair of 1939 was *the* prototype of the up-to-date urban site as a celebration of consumability combined with a modernist faith in the control and possession of the future. The fair had been titled 'Tomorrow's World – Today'. Two and a half decades later and on the other side of the world, Roselands signified that Australia was now Tomorrowland too. With 'everything under one roof', with its environment 'climate-controlled to the temperature of a pleasant Spring day', the complex was as much the physical manifestation of the practices of consumerism as it was of the modernist will to management that had encircled the globe over the previous two centuries. With a media representation of Australian society as a homogenous community of consumption, a community across which the rhetoric of advertising articulated a smooth surface of equality,

135

Roselands allowed the urge to *have it all in one place* a space for expression.

Sydney, a significant manifestation in the nineteenth century of Britain's global reach, had staged an International Exhibition in 1879–1880, which followed the standardised theme of showcasing a comprehensive survey of the products, industry and wealth of Empire. One million people visited the exhibition over the six months it ran, at a time when the combined population of the Australian colonies was only two million.[171] Clearly, the urge to stroll and to look and to marvel within an expansive interior was as well established in Sydney at this time as it was in the arcades of Charles Baudelaire's Paris.[172] The Garden Palace, built in the Domain just off Macquarie Street to house the exhibition, was an impressive construction. Despite being clad in glass and corrugated iron, it was substantially a wooden structure, and, like the Crystal Palace in London from which it was derived, in 1882 it too burnt down. In the nineteenth century the dream of putting everything under the one roof was at best a temporary one, because it was a project that exceeded all available construction technologies.

One hundred years later though, building forms had well and truly caught up with the urge to have it all in one place. In fact, the technologies of steel frame and pre-stressed concrete had turned this dream into a solid and permanent reality. For that part of the Australian population who lived in southwest Sydney, Roselands provided nothing less than a place to 'contemplate the available world' in much the same fashion as, nearly a century earlier, Sydney's labourers and blacksmiths and clerks could stand as cultural if not class equals in the same hall as the *haute bourgeoisie*, surrounded as they all were by the products of *their* Empire. Soon, mega-malls like Roselands would be all over the country, from Indooroopilly in Brisbane to Karrinyup in Perth.

Roselands was said to be 'space age'. By its very nature, a key element of science fiction is a vision of the future, and this is generally either utopian or dystopian. In the West by the middle of the 1960s it was the utopian version that had temporarily triumphed. The dystopian totalitarian potential of modernity, articulated so well by Fritz Lang's 1927 *Metropolis*, appeared to have been conquered, with the liberal bourgeois consumer, rather than the toiling automaton, now the epitome of the totally modern human. Roselands opened while Stanley Kubrick was making *2001: A Space Odyssey*, and it is very much the same ethic of sixties futurism as represented in this epic film – Pan Am space shuttles, zero-gravity air hostesses, and Hilton hotels in orbit about the earth – that finds expression in the media celebrations of Grace Brothers' shopping centre.

The graphic accompanying the *Sydney Morning Herald*'s 'city in the suburbs' story makes this point well, with Roselands drawn as a social and technological space on a par with that most archetypal of modernist locations, the international airport. Citizens dressed in the fashions of the moment bustle, stroll and promenade across the centre court, escalators rise and descend, plants thrive in hanging gardens, and the specially designed fluid slides down the nylon threads of the Raindrop Fountain. The inside has become the outside, while the actual outside is for the moment irrelevant, and Roselands does indeed appear as a self-contained, self-perpetuating environment.

Of crucial importance in this scene is the overall homogeneity of the crowd: an idealised, internationalist middle-class public, with the men all clones of Cary Grant's Roger O. Thornhill from *North by Northwest* (1959), and the women all bobbed and buttoned-down like Jackie Kennedy. Here and there, accompanying children demonstrate that this is very much a place for the heterosexual nuclear family (the ideal social unit of mass consumer society), while both the dress and the facial features of the figures also make plain that this is the preserve of a European race, the fulfillment of the dream of White Australia even as it was being abandoned as official policy. The image perfects the utopian vision of a well-behaved, well-ordered society, the echo of which has been heard ever since. Indeed, in an uncanny foreshadowing of John Howard's 'relaxed and comfortable' Australia of the 1990s, the copy accompanying the drawing tells us that Roselands 'presents new concepts in regional living . . . by the creation of an atmosphere of comfort and relaxation'.[173]

Yet, in much the same manner as in Howard's Australia, the reality of Roselands would never be as antiseptic as the images on the drawing board, because Australian society was shifting and transforming in ways not always under the control of the official managers of change. Look closely at the image, and in the crowd of fashion victims sketched on the floor of the centre court, you'll see two single women, a detail that is as significant within another cultural register as is the racial and socio-economic homogeneity of the rest of the mass. For, as page after page of Grace Brothers' propaganda makes clear, Roselands was very much a woman's space, even more so than a man's. While the origins of this demarcation may have been gendered on traditional lines (the male breadwinner, the female domestic manager/servant), the consequences clearly point elsewhere, as for perhaps the first time in Australian social and cultural history a large and significant public space is dedicated through mainstream media channels as specifically belonging to women and not men.

Fifty years on, daily life in the public space that is still Roselands defies the myth of a homogenous society in which everything was under one roof and under control. Indeed, this process of transgression was underway from the very moment the doors opened in 1965. For example, as testament to the ability of individuals to make use of public space in ways never intended by the planners, it was not long after Roselands opened that it became the location for Sydney's first indoor gay beat. Now, in the twenty first century, it is Roselands' everyday multiculturalism that mocks the celebration of conformity that accompanied its birth. Roselands may have worked to transform the terrain on which it's located (in 1987 Canterbury Council merged segments of the three surrounding suburbs and renamed the new area Roselands), but the surrounding suburbs have also transformed Roselands.

Over the past few decades the character of the local area has changed radically as immigrants from Lebanon, Korea and Vietnam have refashioned the Anglo baby-boom suburban culture celebrated in the opening publicity. Looking down from the same vantage point as that adopted in the 'city in the suburbs' sketch, you see that the crowd is now a highly diverse mixture of styles, attitudes, backgrounds and beliefs. The socio-economic mix is varied too, the wage earners and small business proprietors mixing with the under-employed and the chronically unemployed. Physically, Roselands has changed as well. The Raindrop Fountain is gone, demolished and replaced during the 1980s by a glitzy glass elevator in the Las Vegas style that also, as a further sign of changing attitudes, provides access from floor to floor for the disabled. Part of the centre court has been filled in with more shops, and in the midst of what remains is a Middle Eastern carpet market, the bright reds, blues and oranges of the carpets spreading out in ordered disorder across the tiled floor.

Roselands is no longer the biggest shopping centre in the southern hemisphere. The space age having come and gone, Roselands is now just a rather minor suburban shopping centre with a distinguished past and a very undistinguished present. In the 1980s the title passed to another Sydney complex, Westfield Miranda, an enclosed shopping and entertainment complex built on top of the original Miranda Fair mall, which opened the year before Roselands in 1964. The scale of a second generation mega-mall like Miranda dwarfed the project that was Roselands, while at the same time the rhetoric accompanying such public spaces changed in a subtle but significant way: at Miranda there may have been 'one hundred thousand square metres of retail space, eight cinema screens, an office tower and parking for four and a half thousand cars', and yet, what this added up to wasn't *everything*, but simply 'over three hundred specialty retailers all under the one roof!'[174]

Consumerism had become just too pervasive and too commonplace, too diversified and too segmented for any publicist to attempt to link just one site with the totality of modern life. In 2004 the 'biggest in Australia' title was claimed by Westfield's Bondi Junction complex, a redevelopment of two separate older centres that previously sat on opposite sides of Oxford Street. Now they spread both across the street and underneath it in a segmented development that is as much an adaptation to the existing physical space as it is an imposition upon it. Once again, new technologies were crucial, with the use of computer-driven design and increasingly flexible but durable constructions making possible a form of structure impossible to create in the 1960s. So too with everyday Australian life in general, for, despite the vocal wishes and dreams of conservatives and racists, the era in which it was hoped that 'one people' could make a nation has gone the same way as the claims that one place, one event and one experience could put everything under the 'one roof'.

Despite all this, I have to admit that I still miss the Raindrop Fountain and its promise of a future that never was. Which in turn makes me wonder just how Roselands and the postwar suburban dream it represented should be commemorated? If the images and text on the heritage panel outside the mall are judged to be inadequate because they fail to tell the story of consumer society as it has been played out at this particular spot, then what could be put in their place? In the early 1980s, in *Travels in Hyperreality*, Umberto

Eco asked the question, what are the limits of the media? Did media channels simply advertise products or were they also deeply implicated in those products? Did, for example, the media extend to the crocodile logo on a certain brand of polo shirt?[175] Such an observation prompts more questions, such as, does the media *include* the shirt? What about the place where you buy the shirt? As the pages of Sydney's daily papers celebrating Roselands show, these central aspects of modern social life – information and mediation, style, consumption and exchange – were, and are, clearly and visibly entwined in a complex, contradictory mix of feedback and multiplication.

Perhaps, then, a publicity page from the *Sun-Herald* of 10 October 1965, one displaying a futurist graphic of the climate-controlled complex accompanied by a story detailing all of its intricate, consumable spectacle, should commemorate the coming of Roselands. Or perhaps the heritage panel should display the page on which 'How Hanoi Rides the US Blitz' appeared. After all, Roselands was a massive deployment of modern know-how for a particular purpose at a particular place and time, a deployment that was part of a much bigger narrative, the story of the Cold War, of postcolonialism, and of a multiplicity of global and local operations made possible by the new military and domestic technologies of the 1960s.

Or perhaps the panel should just stay as it is. Maybe its almost total disregard of Roselands as a celebration of shopping is in the end a fitting antidote to the consumerist Year Zero that the arrival of the centre announced. As the newspapers said, Roselands meant *a new way of life*. Few at the time would have argued that the old way of life – inconvenient, under-serviced and uneconomic, concepts which would achieve remarkable influence in all areas of Australian society over the next few decades – wasn't deserving of abolition. But once again, this is only one side of the story. As the old photograph of

Belmore House shows us, the past is a foreign country, and they did things differently there.

7. The Department of Soft Furnishings

At about the same time that the Raindrop Fountain was being installed in the centre of the great city in the suburbs, in the metropolitan centre of Sydney the Hotel Australia was also undergoing a transformation, one designed to bring it 'up-to-date'. If Roselands was Tomorrowland then the Hotel Australia was all about yesterday: it was a celebration of the past, and for the past, at this point in nation's story, there was definitely no future.

Not that those who managed the Hotel Australia saw it that way. The 'Australia' was after all Australia's premier hotel, as its name implied. It was owned and administered by a public company, the Australia Hotel Company and, despite the fact that in the six years between 1960 and 1966 the company's annual operating profit had dropped by 93 percent, there was hope that things could be turned around. Hence the makeover instigated by the Australia's latest manager, Frank Christie, who had been recruited from one of the new, go-ahead international hotels (the Chevron in Potts Point) that had actually taken the Australia's market away and put it into decline.

The remodeling project, timed to coincide with the Hotel's seventy-fifth birthday, was undertaken with no expenses spared. The project was completed late in 1966, having cost $300,000 in the new decimal currency. This was a significant sum of money in the sixties. Little did Frank Christie and the board of the Hotel Australia realise though, that despite their latest investment of capital, their corner of the Central Business District (CBD), which the hotel had occupied since 1891, would soon become the target of a group of developers, architects and engineers who would make both the 'businessmen next door' who made the Taj Mahal, and even the 'men of courage' who built Roselands, look like amateurs.

When the Australia opened in 1891 its first guest was the famed French actress Sarah Bernhardt. Swooned over by the young Marcel in the second part of *À la recherche du temps perdu*, Bernhardt was an early version of the global superstar, and was on a tour of the Australian colonies. Where else would she stay, but at this newest of cosmopolitan locations? Over the years Bernhardt would be followed by luminaries from across the globe and yet, as if to illuminate the direction in which the yet-to-be-federated nation's future lay, the four guestbook entries following that of Bernhardt (who had said she wished that every traveller would 'receive the welcome and feel the same joy' on entering the hotel that she did) were Americans from New York, San Francisco and Detroit.[176]

The building of the Australia had commenced in June 1889, with the laying of the foundation stone presided over by the great manipulator of New South Wales politics, Sir Henry Parkes, in his fifth incarnation as premier. With rhetoric uncannily similar to that which would be used by Robert Askin when commending various big structures built by capitalists three quarters of a century later, Parkes praised the 'boldness of the enterprise'. Grand hotels, he went on, were integral to the progress of modern cities, and with the Australia Hotel complete, Sydney would be able to take its place on the register of great cities of the world.[177] A bottle containing copies of that morning's newspapers (the sort of object that would be known in the space age years of the twentieth century as a 'time capsule') was placed beneath the foundation stone.

Contributors as they were to the Australia's founding moment, Sydney's newspapers were hardly reluctant to share in the celebrations when the hotel opened two years later. The *Herald* went on at length, among other things describing the extensive use of 'white Sicilian' and 'rouge Belgian' marble in the 'grand staircase', the 'remarkable taste and judgement . . . displayed in the magnificent appointments of the dining hall', and the hot and cold running water in the guestrooms.[178]

Such lavish praise was the antecedent to the forms of advertorial boosterism that accompanied developments like Roselands nearly a century later, and it shows us that the state of ecstasy that public relations consultants and journalists seemed to find themselves in when reporting on property development in Sydney in the 1960s actually has a very long history. In fact, the Hotel Australia provided an early instance of the use of that most popular of banal Aussie appellations, *the largest in the southern hemisphere.*[179]

Despite the hype the Australia Hotel, or the Hotel Australia as it was colloquially known, was a key point in the social and cultural map of Sydney. The Australia was a 'bastion of solidity and continuity', writes Carl Ruhen in *Pub Splendid*, his social history of the hotel. 'From its opening until it was demolished eighty years later . . . the Australia was truly the country's premier Grand Hotel with all the luxury and style that this designation implies'.[180] The Australia was home to both transient international celebrities and members of the Australian establishment visiting Sydney. The week of the Royal Easter Show, for example, would find the Australia packed with the squattocracy on their yearly visit to the big smoke. Similarly, 'Polo Week' would crowd the hotel out with members of the rural elite who were even more stuck-up than those who came to town for the Easter Show. In fact, the dining and function rooms played host to countless upper middle-class receptions of one form or another. The heroine of children's writer Mary Grant Bruce's *Billabong Adventurers* (1927), for example, is chided by her best friend for going on a camping trip following her marriage rather than having a proper honeymoon in Sydney at 'The Australia'.[181]

Then there was the Australia's public bar, the Long Bar, which could be entered from Rowe Street. This was a narrow, laneway-width passage that ran between Castlereagh and Pitt Streets, along which the hotel's southern side lay. Lined with art galleries and European-style coffee shops, Rowe Street was positively 'bohemian'. A tourist guide to Sydney in 1882 described the street as composed of 'foreigners' quarters where hurdy gurdy artists, street musicians and others congregate who obtain an uncertain living by such means'. Indeed, one of those who obtained his living so dubiously was a Russian baritone who was accompanied by a dancing bear, with the bear usually being rewarded with a pint of beer at the end of their performance.[182] Nearby on Castlereagh Street was the Theatre Royal, built in 1875 on a site that had previously been occupied by an earlier theatre, the Prince of Wales, dating from the 1850s. By the middle of the twentieth century the Theatre Royal was the last Victorian theatre still standing in central Sydney.

One way or another, a host of disparate groups came together at the Australia. Royal visitors, foreign politicians, international entertainers with big reputations, rural and urban patricians, local radio personalities, journalists, theatregoers and theatre types, painters, poets and students all mingled in the Wintergarden Lounge, to which, according to the Australia's publicity department in 1936, 'everyone who counted in the world found his or her way sooner or later'.[183] The Long Bar, meanwhile, the preserve solely of men in those archaic days of gender-segregated drinking, was usually packed with a mixture of 'respectable' professionals, bohemians from Rowe Street, and off-duty cab drivers. And there was even a place for blokes like the apprentices from Fowler's in Marrickville. Not on a regular basis of course, but for that extra-special celebration. This is why they chose the Australia as the location for their year 2000 reunion, because the Hotel Australia was *the* place, both to be and to be seen in Sydney. Nothing else signified the strength and permanence of modern Australian life like the Hotel Australia.

But things changed a lot over the next thirty years. By 1966 the Hotel Australia, if not exactly on the skids, was certainly struggling. It was losing market share to more modern hotels like the Chevron and the Wentworth, the latter only a couple of blocks away in Elizabeth Street. This situation was not helped by the Australia's refusal to embrace the increasing spread of American popular culture and its ethnically diverse stars, so that Frank Sinatra, Nat King Cole and Louis Armstrong, for instance, were people 'not encouraged' to stay at the Australia.[184] Instead, confronted by the relentless democratisation of the popular, the Australia's answer was to concentrate on what it did best: elitism. Hence the complete overhaul of the hotel's interior, aimed at making it just a little bit groovy and up-to-date while still reinforcing its traditional atmosphere of established conservatism.

The *Sydney Morning Herald* put it this way: 'decorators have aimed for a balanced blend of the hotel's traditional qualities with contemporary decoration features.' Introduced into the Wintergarden, for example, were 'brightly coloured oriental overhead lights' that 'projected an intimate jazz-lounge atmosphere'. This was no doubt the sort of space Sean Connery's James Bond would have found himself at home. The 'relaxed theme' was also 'carried through to the adjoining Terrace Club bar', where 'a rich purple carpet' had been laid, while the actual bar top had been 'softly padded with a toning purple fabric'.[185] And on it went. But perhaps the most remarkable thing about the Australia Hotel's refurbishment – and even the *Herald* thought this remarkable – was that it was a totally in-house operation.

The work had been 'carried out almost entirely by the Hotel's own staff.' This was made possible by the fact that the Australia effectively had on hand its own building company in the form of plumbers, electricians, carpenters, paperhangers, painters and carpet-layers, all organised into their own separate departments. Overall, the renovation was coordinated by the Department of Interior Decorating together with the Department of Soft Furnishings.

Soft Furnishings was headed by 'Miss Margaret McGee', who had, said the *Herald*, 'completed an advanced course in designing and interior decoration in Western Australia before joining the Australia Hotel'. Miss McGee had her work cut out for her, as it was her task to introduce 'a wide range of soft furnishings, including florals, silk brocades, white and cream curtains, distinctive linen spreads, and furniture settings spanning period pieces, classic, provincial and heritage styles'.[186] For all her many responsibilities, she was nonetheless fully up to the job. But in terms of the mechanics of production, such extreme self-reliance on the part of a company seems unimaginable now, after the experience of decades of post-Fordist corporations scouring the globe for the lowest input costs for labour, components and raw materials. And even for an economic entity as small as a stand-alone hotel at the time, it still seems quaintly absurd. And yet, at the Hotel Australia even all the laundry was done in-house by the hotel's own 'extensively appointed' Laundry Department.

By 1966 such wanton refusal to have anything to do with outsourcing or contracting was tantamount to a refusal of the direction in which contemporary capitalism was heading. However, this suited the management of the Australia, much more interested as they were in regaining the glories of the past than embracing those of the present. To this end the publicity surrounding the refurbishment presented the 'Marlene Dietrich Suite' as the Australia's new centerpiece, the most luxuriously renovated room in all the newly renovated hotel and the very same room in fact that the great German *chanteuse* had occupied during her visit to Sydney the previous year. While there was no doubting Dietrich's superstar status, there was also no doubt that her finest hour was behind her. At the height of her fame during the Second World War she'd made the melancholy love song *Lili Marlene* – popular among soldiers on both sides of the barbed wire at El Alamein in 1942 – very much her own. But that was a generation ago. Given the pace of social and cultural change over the intervening decades, it may just as well have been centuries.

The Hotel Australia's board of directors may have been prepared to ignore late modernity, but late modernity wasn't prepared to ignore them. Even at the time the hotel had been built, at the end of the nineteenth century, the block of land it occupied on the corner of King and Castlereagh was a prime piece of real estate. By the 1960s, with office space at a premium in Sydney's CBD, the value of this desirable corner block had gone through the roof. Recall too, that the Australia wasn't a private concern but a public company, and it was extremely vulnerable to a hostile takeover bid. Sizing up the potential of the Australia site were Stocks and Holdings Ltd (owners of the George Adams Hotel in Pitt Street which they would soon redevelop as the Sydney Hilton), the real estate giant LJ Hooker, and the property developer Lend Lease. Also interested, though yet to show its hand, was the big insurer Mutual Life and Citizens Assurance Company Ltd (MLC).

The next few years, from the mid 1960s to the early 1970s, were to witness the most radical transformation of the landscape of central Sydney for at least a century. Mainly due to lobbying by the NSW Fire Brigades, in 1912 restrictions had been introduced limiting the height of Sydney buildings to 150 feet (46 metres). This subsequently ensured that Sydney's aspiring art deco skyscrapers barely exceeded the height of their Victorian predecessors. In 1955 though the Labor premier Joe Cahill had moved to tacitly drop the height limit, and in 1957 a Heights of Buildings Advisory Committee was formed to officially adjudicate on all development proposals for buildings higher than the old limit. Caltex House, a 72-metre steel and concrete structure built in Kent Street in 1957, subsequently became the first International Style office block to be erected in Sydney, while four years later, in 1961, the 117-metre, 31-storey AMP Building at Circular Quay took the mantle of Sydney's first *real* skyscraper.

Joe Cahill was a man who could see the merits of a large concrete structure but, in line with Labor tradition, he tended to favour not the office block but the grand public building, such as his great legacy the Sydney Opera House. In 1959 Cahill died of a heart attack, and was succeeded as premier by the elderly Bob Heffron. In 1964 Heffron retired, and was followed as premier by Jack Renshaw. Labor then lost the state election the next year by one seat to the Liberal-Country Party Coalition, which was led by Robert Askin and backed to the hilt by Sir Frank Packer's *Daily Telegraph*. Askin, as is well known, was partial to development proposals in any shape or form. At this point in Sydney's urban history three separate but powerful forces now converged: the consequences of Cahill's removal of building height restrictions, the pressing need for CBD office space as the Australian economy grew due to the 1960s resource export boom, and the *laissez faire* ideology of the Askin Government. Wiping the slate clean, in 1967 Askin sacked the Sydney City Council and installed a city management commission of three members, chaired by a former head of the NSW Liberal Party, Vernon Hadden Treatt. As far as development proposals were concerned, the commissioners then approved 'whatever was put in front of them'.[187] Property developers, to use the phrase Paul Keating would make his own a few decades later, had never had it so good.

'Sydney is zooming' trumpeted the *Herald* in March 1969, quoting the Premier.[188] This was Askin's response to the announcement of 'an $8 million redevelopment of the Australia Hotel site'. According to the *Herald*, this was the key part of $21 million worth of buildings approved by the Sydney City Commissioners the day before. In the words of one of the commissioners, the previous twelve months had seen 'far more development than in any other similar period – Sydney is really shooting ahead'. Askin, who had entered politics a bank clerk and would leave a millionaire, was never reluctant either to point out the obvious or to laud a good thing when he saw it: 'People only have to look at the towering skyline to notice the dramatic changes that are taking place', he said. 'There has been a record number of building applications and there are more to come.' The commission ruled for twenty-two months and in this time approved $300 million of worth of development projects, which was an awful lot of money in the 1960s. The commission had only ever been an interim measure though, and elections for a new council were held in 1969.[189] Despite growing concerns about the pace of change in some circles, an anti-Labor developers' lobby group marketed as an apolitical set of do-gooder businessmen, the Civic Reform Association, were, as they say, swept to power.

By this point the writing had been on the wall for the Hotel Australia for some time. In December 1967 the *Herald*'s financial editor had surmised that: 'the Australia's days as a hotel must be numbered. Its maximum economic use today would be for office accommodation, no doubt with ground floor shopping in Castlereagh Street and Rowe Street.'[190] Indeed, the Australia's days *were* numbered. Working in a loose alliance, by 1968 MLC and the property developers Lend Lease had acquired 82 percent of the Australia Hotel Company's shares. This was enough for them to take control of the board, propose a redevelopment, and force the sale of the hotel site. On February 25

1970 MLC bought the hotel for $9.6 million, making it the second most expensive piece of land in Sydney. Lend Lease (of which MLC was a major shareholder) then set about acquiring as many nearby properties as possible with the aim of folding the two blocks between Martin Place and King Street and bordered by Castlereagh and Pitt into the one development. In June 1971 Lend Lease announced its development plan, on behalf of MLC, for the site. The Hotel Australia closed on June 30, 1971.

*

In terms of cultural history, the role of Lend Lease in the creation of what would become known as the MLC Centre is significant, for Lend Lease literally embodied so many of the most important urban and commercial developments in New South Wales and Canberra in the second half of the twentieth century. In 1950 Gerardus Dusseldorp was sent to Australia as construction manager of the Dutch building company Bredero's Bouwbedrijf. The young engineer was tasked with finding projects to which Bredero's could contribute, and he quickly tendered for and won a contract from the Snowy Mountains Authority to supply 200 cottages in Cooma for workers on the new Snowy Mountains Scheme.

Bredero's formed a local company, Civil & Civic, to carry out the job, sourcing the prefabricated house frames from Finland, the plumbing from the UK, the roof coverings from Belgium, and the tradesman to put them all together from their own Dutch labour market. It all worked perfectly, an archetype of both the Snowy Mountains Scheme's internationalist methodology and the postwar internationalisation of Australia, exactly the sort of techno-managerial performance that so inspired journalists and writers like George Johnston. By 1953, Dusseldorp, forever more known as Dick courtesy of the dictates of Aussie informality, had become managing director of Civil & Civic.[191]

In 1958 Dusseldorp floated a property development company on the Australian Stock Exchange, Lend Lease, which was designed to create projects that Civil & Civic could then realise. Within three years Lend Lease was so successful that it was able to buy Civil & Civic from Bredero's, with both companies then vertically integrated as an Australian-owned development and production conglomerate. Over the next decade Lend Lease and Civil & Civic were responsible for some of Australia's most significant construction projects: Stage One (the concrete base) of the Sydney Opera House; the hypermodernist Academy of Sciences building in Canberra; Sydney's Caltex House; Canberra's Monaro Mall (which served as the template for Roselands); Bankstown Square (another historic suburban shopping centre development), and the classically internationalist Consolidated Zinc building in Melbourne. Crucially, all these structures were as important in cultural terms as they were in commercial terms. For they were far more than just flash architectural symbols; they demonstrated the extent to which Lend Lease was providing the concrete backbone of postwar Australia, right across the national spectrum, from the great cultural icons, to the fabric of consumerism, to the administration of the mining boom.

In 1958 the architect Harry Seidler, who was known for his radically modernist suburban houses, presented Dusseldorp with a plan for a high-rise residential building in Elizabeth Bay. Dusseldorp liked the project, but insisted on a redesign, and Ithaca Gardens went ahead. In 1959 it won Seidler the Sulman Prize for Architecture. Seidler had been born in Vienna, and left Austria following the *Anschluss* with Nazi Germany in 1938. He'd studied with the Bauhaus founder Walter Gropius at Harvard and worked with the fashionable modernist Oscar Niemeyer in Brazil before settling in Sydney, where his brother already lived. Following their success with Ithaca Gardens, the ongoing design and construction affiliation between Seidler and Associates and Lend Lease would now transform the very look and feel of inner Sydney.

In the early 1960s Lend Lease began buying up and consolidating the separate land titles that made up the city block bordered by George, Pitt, Hunter and Bond Streets. By the end of the decade this site would become Australia Square, a mixture of buildings and public plaza dominated by Seidler's celebrated circular prefabricated concrete office block. The tower was Australia's tallest building on completion in 1968, and the world's tallest lightweight concrete structure, lightweight concrete being a mixture of concrete and light aggregates first developed by Classical Roman builders. It was also topped by the world's largest revolving restaurant. These records were soon surpassed, of course, though the Australia Square tower has remained (at least in my opinion) Australia's most gracefully beautiful building. It was also an immediate commercial success: by early 1969 all fifty floors were occupied by corporate or government tenants.

Almost a parody of the attitudes and practices underpinning the Hotel Australia's refusal of any outside input into its refurbishment, the Lend Lease group had bought up a range of specialist producers in order to supply their grand construction with its key components: a concrete company to manufacture the prefab structural elements, an elevator company, a timber merchant to supply the panels for the internal finish, and so on. The extent to which the development industry in Sydney now owed its allegiance purely to the future rather than to any vestiges of the past could perhaps be judged by the care taken to compile the contents of the time capsule buried by Sydney's mayor, Harry Jensen, in the Square's foundations at the construction commencement ceremony in December 1962. Unlike the prosaic bundle of newspapers placed beneath the Hotel Australia in 1891, the copper cylinder interred under Australia Square provided a far more comprehensive representation of the concerns of Australian modernity. The capsule included a colonial illustration of the site as an open meadow through which a languid Tank Stream flowed, a photograph of the first office building on the site, a collection of Australian pre-decimal coins, a Qantas Airways flight schedule for the day, a Lend Lease brochure, a letter from Jensen addressed to the Lord Mayor of Sydney in 2062, and an essay on 'Life in Sydney' by Cynthia Kaye, a student from Sydney Girls High.[192]

With Australia Square proving such a success, it was inevitable that Lend Lease would soon be looking for another location for an even bigger development, which brings us back to the Hotel Australia. On top of acquiring most of the two desired city blocks, Lend Lease's development of the MLC Centre was further enhanced by Sydney City Council (the new, Civic Reform Association-dominated Council having by this point replaced the City Commissioners) selling them the northern half of Rowe Street to fold into their building ground space. Thus the narrow bohemian enclave was pretty much obliterated, with the remaining portion becoming not much more than laneway access to the new development.

At first Lend Lease had intended to build a new hotel on the site, and Harry Seidler set about planning a building with a hotel in the lower half and office space above. This was for a building that was wider at the top than in the middle, a building with a narrow waist, a structure that would have been one of the world's truly landmark skyscrapers. Unfortunately, due to Lend Lease's anxieties over the financial viability of the combined hotel and office block proposal, it was abandoned in favour of one of Seidler's more straightforward and less radical designs: the brutal and largely uninteresting structure that stands there today. Along with the narrow-waist skyscraper, the hotel proposal went into the bin.

In March 1973 the *Sydney Morning Herald* ran a short article titled 'Making Way for the New'.[193] Accompanying the story was a photograph of a small bulldozer going about its destructive business on top of a pile of rubble on a city street corner. The rubble was, the *Herald* observed, all that remained of the 'once proud fabric of the Australia Hotel'. Months earlier, Australia's largest and longest running auction had disposed of as much of the Australia's internal fittings as was possible. Silverware, crockery, blankets, chandeliers, paintings, statues, ashtrays, carpets, potted plants, even the taps from the Marlene Dietrich Suite went under the hammer to the covetous, the curious and the sentimental.[194] What wasn't sold was then left for the demolishers, and the forlorn remains of Margaret McGee's lovingly selected soft furnishings ended up crunched into the ground under the caterpillar tracks of the industrious little bulldozer.

Despite the efficient pulverising of the Australia, there was still one last gasp of opposition to be heard from the vestiges of Victorian Sydney in this part of town. Following the final performance at the Theatre Royal, a group of emotional and nostalgic thespians decided to mount a challenge to the venue's demolition. They approached Jack Mundey, head of the Builders Labourers Federation (BLF) trade union, and asked him to place a Green Ban on the site on account of its historical and cultural significance. And he did. This was a remarkable period in the history of both social protest and industrial relations in Australia. By the early 1970s, with no governmental bodies either up to or desiring the task, the BLF had become the unofficial protector of Sydney's natural and cultural heritage.[195] Under Jack Mundey's socially aware, politically-conscious and committed leadership, the BLF had joined forces over the previous couple of years with a range of middle-class home-owner, student and activist groups to prevent some of the more extreme proposals coming out of Sydney's rampant property development drive from going ahead. Mundey had refashioned the industrial action device of the 'Black Ban' into the 'Green Ban', citing environmental factors and issues in order to impose work bans on any project deemed socially undesirable by the BLF and the activists with whom it was collaborating. This was a very successful tactic, and while it is only a distant memory now (after the wholesale abolition of so much of Australian workers' rights and power by the Howard and Abbott governments), back then, if the BLF said a project was not going to go ahead, well then it didn't go ahead. It was as simple as that.

When work had commenced on Australia Square a decade earlier, Lend Lease had been allowed to divert the Tank Stream, which flowed directly under the site, around the project. The stream, which had provided the first water source for colonial Sydney, was encased in convict era brickwork, and yet no one had even batted an eyelid at this vandalism. Now, thanks to the industrial clout of the BLF, an old theatre, which almost everyone involved agreed was of no real architectural value, was to be defended for cultural reasons alone.

The issue was, however, quickly resolved. For one thing, the BLF had developed an excellent working relationship with Dusseldorp and the management of Civil & Civic, who realised that cooperating with the union movement was by far the best way of getting what they wanted efficiently and safely. As soon as the Theatre Royal Green Ban was announced, two public meetings were organised to rally support for the resistance to demolition. Despite a hostile reception, Dusseldorp fronted both meetings and declared that if it would make everyone happy, then Lend Lease would incorporate a new theatre into the MLC project. Seidler was given two weeks (which anyone who has patronised the place will probably agree wasn't long enough, not even for Seidler) to take care of this detail, and the Green Ban was lifted. The demolishers then went back to work on the future MLC site, while the anger of the Theatre Royal sentimentalists was mostly mollified. Yet nobody had come forward to speak out for that former domicile of toffs, cosmopolitans, bohemians and interior decorators that was the Hotel Australia.

On the first day of August 1972 the *Herald* reported that the Sydney City Council 'yesterday approved plans for Sydney's tallest building – the $70 million, 750 foot office tower on the Hotel Australia site'. This was the final design for the site, incorporating a new Theatre Royal. As with the early publicity for Roselands, the usual bunch of public amenities were trotted out as essential parts of the development in order to justify it in civic terms. According to the *Herald*, the '60 storey project' would include, as well as a 'live theatre', a 'branch public library, shopping arcades, a restaurant, a child-minding centre, and extensive public areas.' All in all, developers, protestors and councilors seemed happy with the outcome. The *Herald* continued: 'The octagonal-shaped building, which will dominate the city's skyline, was described by the Chairman of the City Development Committee, Alderman A. Briger, as 'probably the last of the city's very tall buildings'.[196] This was perhaps the silliest remark in the entire history of civic planning in Australia.

The obliteration of the Hotel Australia is the climax of the story of the self-made man, of the postwar imperative to build, to develop, and to make it all new. The irresistible processes of internationalisation and modernization given form in the twin phenomena of the great immigration program and the development of the minerals export economy found their terminal points of realisation in the lightweight concrete skyscrapers rising all over central Sydney by the end of the 1960s. Meanwhile, the ethics of progress provided the belief system holding it all together. Like all climaxes though, this one was as destructive as it was productive, as the structures that the spirit of the self-made man had built, and now inhabited, had moved far beyond the scope or control of any single individual. As the Sydney-based Romanian-Australian cartoonist, academic, and architectural critic George Molnar was to put it, commenting as much on the global as the local spirit of contemporary design, architecture had lost its human scale.[197]

A *Sydney Morning Herald* editorial on the day after the final plans for the MLC Centre were approved by council addressed the same concerns:

> The rebuilding, or, if you like, the destruction of Old Sydney is continuing apace . . . Where will it all end? Will Sydney be a more beautiful and exciting city with its new buildings? Many people doubt it. A living city must continue renewing itself. But it must be careful that it does not do so at the expense of destroying buildings of historic or architectural interest and regions of special atmosphere that give the city its character.[198]

The *Herald* leader writer had hit upon the key issue in this brief and eloquent passage: we need to take care of our social and cultural history. Yet the forces of progress and development propelling Australia at this time made such care pretty well impossible. These ideals were all about looking forward, not looking back. As Dennis had explained to Nino when they were digging trenches in Punchbowl in the 1950s, the self-made man had no use at all for introspection or reflection. He just had to get on with the job, because the here and now of the job was all there was.

In Sydney by the end of the 1960s, the ideologies of progress and development were out of control. Indeed, driven by the intertwined imperatives of exploitation and accumulation, they had never really been much under control in the first place. And yet it had all seemed so manageable, so containable and so benign a couple of decades earlier: just one more block of land to clear, one more house frame to put up, and then Joe and his small group of non-unionised mates could have a barbecue, a few beers, and a bit of a laugh. But, as George Molnar indicated, by the early 1970s the scale of this world had changed out of all proportion. Nino the spec builder had given way to Dick Dusseldorp, and Joe's little company had morphed into Lend Lease. By now the issues of production were so complex that they were best chronicled by accountants rather than by comic novelists. On the MLC Centre project, for example, in addition to their subsidiary production companies initially acquired to build Australia Square, Lend Lease had employed a further one hundred subcontractors, each of whom in turn had employed teams of tradesmen and labourers.[199] In this environment the individualist self-made man was no hero anymore, he was just a name on a payroll collecting a pay packet at the end of the week.

We shouldn't get too sentimental about this, though. Of course from a romantic point of view we could see this progression as a melancholy allegory of the destructive impact of the impersonal processes of late modernity: the worlds of both the fair dinkum self-employed builder and the well-mannered, old-style patrician both swallowed up by the ravenous appetite of an internationalised property development conglomerate. But this isn't really how it was. Rather, it was all a question of scale. Because to a great extent Dusseldorp and Seidler's visions were, while an awful lot bigger, just as pure as Nino Culotta's or Stan Parker's. They each wanted to clear away what had come before in order to make something new, something they saw as not just new but also better. For Dusseldorp and Seidler it was old buildings, for Nino and Stan it was virgin bush and scrub.

In terms of the organising of daily life, the ideologies of progress and development made possible the actions of all these characters, both fictional and non-fictional. And ultimately, it was not some mythical 'end of an era' that brought about the destruction of the Hotel Australia. It was the very same beliefs and values – the 'boldness of the enterprise' — that Sir Henry Parkes had lauded on the day he laid its foundation stone in 1891.

8. He Feared No Man

In the 1970s a one-armed man sold peanuts to the crowd at Kogarah Oval on the days St George played their home games there. I call him a one-armed man, though he still possessed most of his left arm, which ended as a skinny stump wrapped in a brown bandage about halfway between his elbow and the space where his hand should have been. This stump was actually very useful: he carried on it an old leather shopping bag containing his small packets of nuts, and he made his way through the crowd, whether large or small, in sunshine or rain, selling his wares to the momentarily distracted fans. His bag contained three types of nuts. 'In the shell or sugar-coated twenty cents, cashews are forty', were the only words he spoke, and he repeated them continuously, like a newspaper vendor calling out a headline, or a Tibetan monk chanting a mantra: 'In the shell or sugar-coated twenty cents, cashews are forty. In the shell or sugar-coated twenty cents, cashews are forty. In the shell . . . '

Whenever I think about the football games of the 1970s, this stooped old man with his gravelly voice, his leathery face, and a bag of packaged nuts dangling from his stumpy arm is my most vivid memory, much more memorable than any particular game of rugby league, or any particular footballer. Years later my friend Stephen Parry – Pazza, we called him – would often amuse us by spontaneously repeating the words 'In the shell or sugar-coated twenty cents, cashews are forty', in comic imitation of the one-armed peanut seller. He never needed to explain the reference: if you'd been at Kogarah Oval in those days you would get it, and if you hadn't, well it didn't matter anyway.

Pazza was good at impersonations. Another character he liked to take off on a regular basis was Jack the Bus. Jack had earned this appellation because he worked as a bus driver. Most evenings at the end of the 1970s, after he finished his shift, and still wearing his uniform, he would sit at a small, round laminex table in the public bar of the Arncliffe Hotel and drink schooner after schooner of beer. And after a while he too, like the one-armed peanut seller, would begin to chant a sort of mantra: 'Johnny Raper, Johnny Raper . . . he feared no man, he feared no man', he would repeat, over and over again. Of course, all Pazza had to do to reduce his audience to tears of laughter was utter the words 'he feared no man' at a particularly opportune moment.

Johnny Raper had been St George's lock forward during the glory years, and he was famous for his incisive, bone-crunching cover tackles, his ruthless courage in attack, and his reckless and riotous off-field drinking bouts and generally ribald behavior. Maybe it is true, maybe Johnny Raper did fear no other man. I don't know, but I'm much more sure of the fact that Jack the Bus feared many men, as most of us do, but that he found in his inebriated homage to the fearless Johnny an inkling of the courage he needed to battle his own way forward, day after day.

I have my own memories of the era of the self-made man, but they're the vague memories of childhood. By the time I'd grown old enough to begin to formulate my own views on the world around me, this most influential of times was over. I can only clearly recall its detritus: the stooped old man with his bag of peanuts, Jack the Bus with his wounded nostalgia, and also, my mate Kevin and I, despite being underage, frequenting a basement bar at Martin Place that was dug into the ground directly under the MLC tower. In deference to the once-famous landmark that had stood on that spot, the bar was called the Australia Tavern, but at the time both the reference and the irony were largely lost on us. Like its namesake, this bar also eventually disappeared, with the underground space becoming a cinema for a couple of decades, and later an outlet for a retail chain specialising in computer accessories and cheap electronics.

Brewer's Dictionary of Phrase and Fable defines a self-made man as 'one who has risen from poverty and obscurity to comparative opulence or a position of importance by his own efforts'.[200] In this sense Australia, like the United States, is one of the world's prime locations for such a figure. As A.G.L. Shaw, one of the pillars of twentieth-century Australian historiography, put it in 1960, in social terms the 'most important feature' of Australia at this time was 'the absence of a wealthy leisured ruling class, bred in aristocratic tradition, attending to public service as well to private interest'.[201] Shaw went on to ponder whether or not such a group actually existed anywhere apart from in 'the minds of idealistic conservatives'. This was a question that he felt was insoluble. The only real certainty, Shaw argued, was that without a doubt this particular social group didn't exist in Australia.

An understanding of Australia such as this, a place devoid of a rigid and defining cultural and material inheritance, was crucial to the creation, the spread and the influence of the image of the self-made man. For the social and cultural space the self-made man occupied was essentially a blank space. With no burden of history upon him (as this was a burden which was thought to have been left behind in Europe), and with no economic capital at his disposal (apart from that which he could make from nothing with his own two hands), the self-made man was compelled to recreate the world anew in this new land, and recreate it in nobody's image but his own.

Like all national narratives, this was, this is, a fiction. In reality history weighed on the mind of the self-made man just as it did, just as it does, on the minds of every other human alive. In his case it was the history of European imperialism, of the dispossession of the Aborigines over here and of the Irish and Scots back there, of the careless exploitation of the land and its resources, of the destruction of much of Europe by fascism, and of the need for millions of ethnically diverse refugees to find new lives. Yet, despite the presence of all this history, out among the land clearance and the concreting and the bricklaying, in suburb after suburb of endless new development, it must have seemed, for a while at least, as if the self-made man was really starting out from scratch.[202]

This is the point where the story of the self-made man intersects most closely with that most exemplary of twentieth-century narratives: the fable of relentless, unrestrained progress. This in turn is the story, both personal and national, that allowed the three young apprentices at Fowler Potteries in the 1930s to imagine themselves more than six decades later, affirming their existence and their staying power, in the Long Bar of the Hotel Australia. And this is, of course, also the very same story that took their utopia away from them.

Endnotes

1   Zygmunt Baumann, 'Introduction: The Quest for Order', in *Modernity and Ambivalence*, Polity Press, Cambridge, 1991, 1–17.

2   Hannah Arendt, 'Introduction: Walter Benjamin: 1892–1940', Walter Benjamin, *Illuminations*, trans. Harry Zohn, ed. Arendt, Shocken Books, New York, 1968, 11.

3   Ibid.

4   David Meredith and Barrie Dyster, *Australia in the Global Economy: Continuity and Change*, Cambridge University Press, Cambridge, 1999, 195, 271.

5   Walter Benjamin, trans. Harry Zohn, 'The Paris of the Second Empire in Baudelaire', *Charles Baudelaire: A Lyric Poet in the Era of High Capitalism*, Verso, London, 1973, 36: 'the *flâneur* who goes botanizing on the asphalt'.

6   Patrick White, *Voss*, Eyre & Spottiswoode, London, 1957, 235.

7   David Marr, *Patrick White: A Life*, Vintage, Milsons Point, 1992, 379.

8   Ibid., 323.

9   Ibid., 323.

10 Quoted in Jane Clark and Bridget Whitelaw, *Golden Summers, Heidelberg and Beyond*, International Cultural Corporation of Australia, Melbourne, 1985, 149.

11 *Age*, 16 August 1905, 6.

12 Patrick White, *The Tree of Man*, Viking, New York, 1955, 1.

13 Patrick White, 'The Prodigal Son', *Australian Letters* 1.3 (1958), 39.

14 Marr, 275, 282.

15 White, *The Tree of Man*, 394.

16 Tim Rowse, *Australian Liberalism and National Character*, Kibble, Melbourne, 1978, 233.

17 Marjorie Barnard, 'The Four Novels of Patrick White', *Meanjin* 15.2 (1956), 165.

18 Katharine Susannah Prichard, 'Comment', *Overland* 13 (October 1958), 14.

19 Gilberto Freyre, *New World in the Tropics: The Culture of Modern Brazil*, Alfred A. Knopf, New York, 1959. Almost all of Freyre's work deals with this issue in one way or another, but this particular book provides a concise overview of his ideas.

20 Quoted in Rowse, 235.

21 C.M.H. (Manning) Clark, *A History of Australia, Volume 4: The Earth Abideth Forever 1851–1888*, Melbourne University Press, Carlton, 1978, 176.

22 Peter Doyle, *The Devil's Jump*, Random House, Milsons Point, 2001, 105–6.

23 John O'Grady, pseud. Nino Culotta, *They're a Weird Mob*, Ure Smith, Sydney, 1974 (1957), 33.

24 'Real Estate', *Daily Telegraph*, 20 July 1963, 11.

25 David Carter, 'O'Grady, John *see* Culotta, Nino: Popular Authorship, Duplicity and Celebrity', *Australian Literary Studies* 21.4 (2004), 56.

26 O'Grady, 1.

27 Italo Calvino, trans. William Weaver, *If On a Winter's Night a Traveller*, Picador, London, 1982, 3.

28 Donald Horne, *The Lucky Country*, Penguin, Ringwood, 1964, 22.

29 Ibid.

30 Robin Boyd, 'The Look of Australia', in Peter Coleman, ed. *Australian Civilization: A Symposium*, Cheshire, Melbourne, 1962, 76.

31 Horne, 17.

32 Ibid., 9.

33 O'Grady, 40.

34 Ibid., 26.

35 Ibid., 36.

36 Frederick Eggleston, 'The Australian Nation' in George Caiger ed., *The Australian Way of Life*, Heinemann, London, 1953, 14.

37 Dorothy Hewett, *Bobbin Up* (1958), Virago, London, 1985, 74.

38 O'Grady, 12.

39 Cited in Brian Murphy, *The Other Australia: Experiences of Migration*, Cambridge University Press, Cambridge, 1993, 157.

40 Richard Bosworth, *Cop What Lot?: A Study of Australian Attitudes Towards Italian Mass Migration in the 1950s*, Catholic Intercultural Resource Centre, North Fitzroy, 1986, 6.

41 Bosworth, 6.

42 O'Grady, 35.

43 J.L. Austin, *How to Do Things With Words*, 2nd ed., Oxford University Press, Oxford, 1975, 5–6.

44 O'Grady, 15.

45 Ibid., 57.

46 Ibid., 44.

47 Ibid., 202.
48 Ibid., 204.
49 Murphy, *The Other Australia*, 107.
50 Cited in Carter, 62.
51 Thanks very much to Liliana Zavaglia for telling me about Salvatore Tripodi and the *cantastorie* in Australia.
52 Gitano Rando, 'Expressions of the Calabrian Diaspora in Australian Writing', Proceedings of Minorities and Cultural Assertions – Literary and Social Diasporas Conference, University of Wollongong, 8–10 October 2004, available at http://ro.uow.edu.au/artspapers/20 (accessed on 12 January 2014).
53 Michael Hulse, introduction to Johann Wolfgang von Goethe, *The Sorrows of Young Werther*, Penguin, London, 1989, 16.
54 O'Grady, 205.
55 Cited in Bosworth, 13.
56 See, for example, 'That familiar mushroom over Maralinga again', *Sun-Herald*, 10 October 1957, 3. The story carried a photograph of Britain's most recent nuclear bomb test, said by the caption to be a 'familiar' image.
57 ' "A-Bomb" Rocks Jungle in Army's Cape York Test', *Sydney Morning Herald*, 19 July 1963, 1.
58 Ibid.
59 For one of many, many accounts of this period, see Robert Dallek, *An Unfinished Life: John F. Kennedy, 1917–1963*, Little, Brown & Co., Boston, 2003.
60 Graham Freudenberg, *A Figure of Speech: A Political Memoir*, John Wiley & Sons, Milton, 2005, 31.
61 Alan Reid, 'Waiting for Instructions . . . from Their Bosses – Leaders or Office boys?', *Daily Telegraph*, 22 March 1963, 5. Reid had once been a member of the ALP, but had been expelled.
62 Alan Reid, *Daily Telegraph*, 6 March 1963, 10; 16 March 1963, 1.
63 Alan Reid, 'Leaders or Office boys?', *Daily Telegraph*, 22 March 1963, 5.
64 Alan Reid, 'Pro-Reds, Leftists tell Calwell what to do', *Sunday Telegraph*, 24 March 1963, 3.
65 Shirley Purchase, *Canberra's Early Hotels: A Pint-Sized History*, Canberra & District Historical Society, Canberra, 1999, 118.
66 'Who will you trust to govern Australia', Liberal Party election advertisement, *Daily Telegraph*, 26 November 1963, 13.
67 Gilles Deleuze and Félix Guattari, trans. Brian Massumi, *A Thousand Plateaus: Capitalism and Schizophrenia*, University of Minnesota Press, Minneapolis, 1987, 181.
68 Ian Heads, *March of the Dragons: The Story of St George Rugby League Club*, Lester-Townsend Publishing, Sydney, 1989, 90.

69 *St George Call*, 4 July 1963, 1.

70 Heads, 90.

71 Cited in Andrew Moore, *The Mighty Bears!: A Social History of North Sydney Rugby League*, Macmillan, Sydney, 1996, 268.

72 Annual report of the North Sydney Rugby League Football Club, 1956, cited in Moore, 271.

73 According to my father, Arthur Barrett.

74 Heads, 90.

75 Moore, 411–12.

76 Ken Inglis, assisted by Jan Brazier, *Sacred Places: War Memorials in the Australian Landscape*, Melbourne University Press, Carlton, 2005, 458–71.

77 See Clark, *A History of Australia, Volume 4: The Earth Abideth Forever 1851–1888*, chapter 12, 'The Kingdom of Nothingness'.

78 Inglis, 460–461.

79 Clark, *A History of Australia, Volume 5: The People Make Laws 1888–1915*, Melbourne University Press, Carlton, 1981, 359.

80 Foyer description in 'Building Today', *Daily Telegraph*, 1 July 1963, 21.

81 Information on the Campbell portrait supplied by St George Leagues Club management.

82 Heads, 79.

83 Norm Provan, foreword to Heads, *March of the Dragons*, 7.

84 *Daily Mirror*, 1 July 1963, 35.

85 'Eleven Years in the Melting Pot', *Daily Mirror*, 1 July 1963, 35.

86 'Club's Secret is Teamwork', *Daily Mirror*, 1 July 1963, 34.

87 Heads, 30.

88 Heads, 105.

89 Ibid.

90 *Daily Mirror*, 1 July 1963, 34.

91 See 'Introduction: Rhizome', in Gilles Deleuze and Felix Guattari, *A Thousand Plateaus: Capitalism and Schizophrenia*, Bloomsbury, London, 2013, 1–27.

92 'Sydney Town', *Sun-Herald*, 21 July 1963, 96.

93 'He's got top US contract', *Sunday Telegraph*, 21 July 1963, 13.

94 The St George district was at the time also home to the Francis Drake Bowling Club at Monterey, and the Elizabethan Women's Bowling Club at Rockdale.

95 Cited in Heads, 96.

96 General Motors Holden advertisement, *Meanjin Quarterly*, 1.23 (1964), inside back cover.

97 Horne, 17.

98 An avowed modernist, Dadswell appeared for the defence in the infamous trial over the award of the 1943 Archibald Prize to William Dobell for his

portrait of fellow artist Joshua Smith: see Richard Haese, *Rebels and Precursors: The Revolutionary Years of Australian Art*, Penguin, Ringwood, 1988, 226–227.

99 Clem Christensen, 'Trailer: More About the Libraries Scandal', *Meanjin Quarterly*, 1.23 (1964), 112.

100 Raymond Williams, 'Base and Superstructure in Marxist Cultural Theory', *Problems in Materialism and Culture: Selected Essays*, Verso, London, 1980, 38.

101 The 'media' as a set of systems and practices that are both produced by and produce meaning in a society, particularly a society based on individual consumption, is indeed a difficult 'object' to define.

102 Martin Boyd, 'Dubious Cartography', *Meanjin Quarterly* 1.23 (1964), 7.

103 '*Indonesia* by Bruce Grant' (advertisement), *Meanjin Quarterly*, 1.23 (1964), 92.

104 'The Coonawarra Estate' (advertisement), ibid., inside front cover.

105 The advertisement in question is interpreted as an example of a 'closed' text as defined by Umberto Eco. It doesn't demand a great deal of input from the reader/consumer in order to interpret the meaning, but instead announces a relatively straightforward, unproblematic argument. See *The Role of the Reader: Explorations in the Semiotics of Texts*, Indiana University Press, Bloomington, 1979.

106 Philip Murphy, *What is Wine?*, Allen & Unwin, St Leonards, 2000, 18.

107 O'Grady, *Cop This Lot* (1960), Child & Henry, Brookvale, 1987, 210.

108 Ibid., 15.

109 Ibid., 110.

110 James Halliday, *Coonawarra: The History, the Vignerons & the Wines*, Yenisey, Sydney, 1983, 81. Wynn is the 'Australianised' form of Weintraub. When Samuel Wynn (1891–1982) arrived in Australia in 1913, the Immigration Officer interviewing him was unable to cope with his Polish surname and so wrote down Wynn on his documents: a great example of Australia's assimilationist ethnic and cultural policies up to and including the 1950s.

111 Ibid.

112 Pierre Bourdieu, trans. Richard Nice, *Distinction: A Social Critique of the Judgement of Taste*, Harvard University Press, Cambridge, Mass., 1984, 170.

113 Ibid., 175.

114 Ibid., 466–68.

115 Anne Bavinton, 'The Darkness of Brennan's "Lilith"', *Meanjin Quarterly*, 1.23 (1964), 63–69.

116 George Johnston, *Clean Straw for Nothing*, Collins, London and Sydney 1969, 99.

117 O'Grady, *They're a Weird Mob*, 1.

118 CRA advertisement, *Meanjin Quarterly* 1.23 (1964), 1.

119 Deleuze and Guattari, 95.

120 William J. Lines, *Taming the Great South Land: A History of the Conquest of Nature in Australia*, Allen and Unwin, North Sydney 1991, 203.

121 Cited in J. Roberts and D. McLean, *The Cape York Aluminium Companies and the Native Peoples: Alcan, Comalco, R.T.Z., Kaiser, C.R.A., Billiton, Pechiney, Tipperary* (Mapoon – Book Three), International Development Action, Fitzroy, 1976, 10.

122 Lines, 204.

123 An example of how much this particular economic and politically generated state of affairs was understood by those in power as a natural, commonsense view of the world came in November 1977 when Bjelke-Petersen was interrogated by the ABC television program *Four Corners* on the subject. In relation to a question by Paul Lyneham on possible conflicts of interest arising from the State Premier being financially involved in minerals exploration and exploitation, the politician replied in his characteristic semi-articulate but aggressive style: 'Well, would . . . would . . . would you . . . you want to have a Premier who had never achieved anything?' *Four Corners*, 'Utah and Australia', ABC Television, 4 November 1977, http://www.abc.net.au/4corners/stories/2011/08/08/3288475.htm, (19 February 2014).

124 W.H. Blackmore, M.J. Elliot and R.E. Cotter, *Landmarks: A History of Australia to the Present Day*, Macmillian, South Melbourne, 1969, 211.

125 John Bellair, 'The Man Who was Different', *Meanjin Quarterly*, 1.23 (1964), 61.

126 Benedict Anderson, *Imagined Communities: Reflections on the Origin and Spread of Nationalism*, rev. ed., Verso, London, 1991.

127 Walter Benjamin 'Eduard Fuchs, Collector and Historian', in Howard Eiland and Michael W. Jennings, eds., *Walter Benjamin: Selected Writings, Volume 3: 1935–1938*, Harvard University Press, Cambridge, Mass., 2002, 267.

128 Cited in Benjamin, 'Eduard Fuchs', 283.

129 Benjamin, 'Eduard Fuchs', 267.

130 CRA advertisement, *Meanjin Quarterly* 1.23 (1964), 1.

131 Benjamin, 'Eduard Fuchs', 267.

132 'The SMH Roselands Feature', *Sydney Morning Herald*, 12 October 1965, 1.

133 Lindsay Tanner, *Open Australia*, Pluto Press, Annandale, 1999, 17.

134 *Daily Telegraph*, 9 September 1965, 42.

135 'Roselands Supplement', *Daily Mirror*, 11 October 1965, 30.

136 'There's Fizz in the air', *Sun*, 11 October 1965, 26.

137 'Askin opens £6m. Retail Centre, *Sydney Morning Herald*, 12 October 1965, 4.

138 Gustave Flaubert, trans. Geoffrey Wall, *Madame Bovary: Provincial Lives*, Penguin, London, 2003, 143.

139 *Get to Know Trend-Setting Roselands*, Grace Brothers publicity pamphlet, 1965.

140 'Praise for workmen', *Daily Mirror*, 11 October 1965, 26.

171

141 'Vision and £6m creates "city" in suburbs', Roselands Feature, *Sydney Morning Herald*, 12 October 1965, 1.

142 'Ads on TV annoy PM', *Daily Mirror*, 11 October 1965, 11. Playing for laughs as always, Menzies bemoaned the impact of advertising on his recreational television viewing: 'Just when Simon Templar is about to nab a gang of crooks a woman comes dancing onto the screen and begins to hang her washing in the main street.' Graham Freudenberg always thought Menzies had no need for a speechwriter, and maybe he was right: here Ming manages to depict in a single image both the (for him) triviality of working-class women's concerns and his perpetual love of pseudo-toffs like Roger Moore.

143 *Sun-Herald*, 10 October 1965, 52.

144 'Roselands—A Sydney Morning Herald Feature', *Sydney Morning Herald*, 12 October 1965, 1.

145 'Bazaar-like Centre Court dazzles with colour and excitement', Roselands Feature, *Sydney Morning Herald*, 12 October 1965, 2.

146 Ibid., 1.

147 'A Garden City in the suburbs', *Sun-Herald*, 10 October 1965, 46.

148 'Ideas Men Give Centre Character', *Daily Telegraph*, 12 October 1965, 34.

149 John Casazza and Frank Spink, *The Shopping Centre Development Handbook*, The Urban Land Institute, Washington, DC, 1985, 13.

150 Roselands Feature, *Sydney Morning Herald*, 12 October 1965, 1.

151 This information provided by George Gittoes in conversation.

152 'Television will end parents' worries', Roselands Feature, *Sydney Morning Herald*, 12 October 1965, 2.

153 Many thanks to Sylvia Lawson (1932-2017) for this observation. Sylvia made the point (in conversation) that in 1965 child-minding services were available for mothers who wanted to shop but not for those who wanted to go to the library.

154 'Indo Mob's Anger', *Daily Mirror*, 11 October 1965, 1.

155 'How Hanoi Rides the US Blitz', *Sun-Herald*, 10 October 1965, 89.

156 'Jet "dogfights" give Sydney the shudders', *Sydney Morning Herald*, 12 October 1965, 1.

157 John Updike, 'Rabbit Redux' (1971) in *A Rabbit Omnibus*, London, Penguin, 1991, 206.

158 *The Roselands Story*, Coles-Myer publicity pamphlet, 1989.

159 'It's Australia's biggest store', *Daily Mirror*, 5 October 1965, 7.

160 Charles Jencks, *The Language of Post-Modern Architecture*, Rizzoli, New York, 1981, 37.

161 Daniel Miller, *Material Culture and Mass Consumption*, Basil Blackwell, Oxford, 1987, 204.

162 Meaghan Morris, 'Things To Do With Shopping Centres', in Susan Sheridan,

ed., *Grafts: Feminist Cultural Criticism*, Verso, London, 1988, 222.

163 'The Soup-Can Artist', *Sun-Herald*, 10 October 1965, 78.

164 Patterson Sims, cited in Victor Bockris, *Warhol*, Muller, London, 1989, 145.

165 Thomas Crow, 'Saturday Disasters' in Serge Guilbaut, ed., *Reconstructing Modernism: Art in NewYork, Paris and Montreal, 1945–1964*, MIT Press, Cambridge, Mass., 1990, 324.

166 Robert Hughes, *Nothing If Not Critical*, Collins-Harvill, London, 1990, 244.

167 Warhol, cited in Bockris, 155, 170.

168 Jean Baudrillard, 'Consumer Society', in *Jean Baudrillard: SelectedWritings*, ed. Mark Poster, Polity, Cambridge, 1989, 34, 49.

169 'Roselands Feature' *Sydney Morning Herald*, 12 October 1965, 2.

170 Paul Greenhalgh, *Ephemeral vistas: the expositions universelles, great exhibitions, and world's fairs, 1851–1939*, Manchester University Press, Manchester, 1988, 23–24.

171 Henry J. Cowan, *FromWattle & Daub to Concrete & Steel:The Engineering Heritage of Australia's Buildings*, Melbourne University Press, Carlton South, 1998, 56.

172 See Benjamin, *Charles Baudelaire: A Lyric Poet in the Era of High Capitalism*.

173 Roselands Feature, *Sydney Morning Herald*, 12 October 1965, 1.

174 *Directory and Services Guide —Westfield Shoppingtown Miranda*, publicity pamphlet, February 1997.

175 Umberto Eco, trans. William Weaver, 'The Multiplication of the Media' in *Travels in Hyperreality: Essays*, Picador, London, 1987, 148–49.

176 Carl Ruhen, *Pub Splendid:The Australia Hotel, 1891–1971*, John Burrell in association with Murray Child & Company, Collaroy, 1995, 23.

177 Ibid., 16.

178 'The Australia Hotel', *Sydney Morning Herald*, 20 June 1889, 7.

179 'The Australia Hotel—Laying of the Corner Stone', *Sydney Morning Herald*, 19 June 1889, 4.

180 Ruhen, 9–10.

181 Mary Grant Bruce, *Billabong Adventurers*, Ward, Lock, Melbourne, 1974, 16.

182 Ruhen, 24.

183 Ibid., 28

184 Ibid., 80

185 'Australia Hotel remodeled for 75th birthday', *Sydney Morning Herald*, 1 November 1966, 14.

186 Ibid.

187 Architect-planner George Clarke, cited in Elizabeth Farrelly, 'Storeys with a Happy Ending', *Sydney Morning Herald*, 16–17 July 2005, Spectrum 27.

188 'Approval for $21m of city growth', *Sydney Morning Herald*, 11 March 1969, 1.

189 Leonie Sandercock, *Cities for Sale: Property, Politics and Urban Planning in Australia*, Melbourne University Press, Carlton, 1975, 197.

190 'The Australia and the Stock Exchange', *Sydney Morning Herald*, 5 December 1967, 22.

191 There is a detailed account of these events in Lindie Clark, *Finding a Common Interest: The Story of Dick Dusseldorp and Lend Lease*, Cambridge University Press, Cambridge, 2002.

192 Mary Murphy, *Challenges of Change: The Lend Lease Story*, Lend Lease, Sydney, 1984, 84.

193 'Making Way for the New', *Sydney Morning Herald*, 9 March 1972, 16.

194 Ruhen, 130.

195 Clark, *Finding a Common Interest*, 156.

196 'Sydney's Tallest Building Cleared', *Sydney Morning Herald*, 1 August 1972, 3.

197 George Molnar, 'Human Scale in Architecture', *Architecture Australia*, 5.68 (1979), 30–37.

198 'New Face of Sydney', *Sydney Morning Herald*, 2 August 1972, 6.

199 Murphy, *Challenges of Change*, 134.

200 *Brewers Dictionary of Phrase and Fable*, ed. Ivor H. Evans, Cassell, London, 1990, 997.

201 A.G.L. Shaw, *The Story of Australia*, Faber & Faber, London, 1960, 271.

202 This creation of capital from the dispossession of a colonised people is a prime example of what Rosa Luxemburg understood as primitive accumulation of capital. See Rosa Luxemburg, 'The Historical Conditions of Accumulation', in *The Rosa Luxemburg Reader*, eds. Peter Hudis and Kevin B. Anderson, The Monthly Review Press, New York, 2004. 32–70.

www.ingramcontent.com/pod-product-compliance
Lightning Source LLC
Chambersburg PA
CBHW030831090426
42737CB00009B/962